D0611894

In a world where it seems everything is con. presents simple yet profound parenting wisdom that can empower parents at all stages of life to embrace their God-given role with fresh zeal and confidence. The book is packed with biblically based relational truths that are doable and day-to-day smart yet miraculously life changing. If you want to touch the future by preparing your children for life with God, read the Bible and this book.

Ivey Harrington Beckman
Editor in Chief
HomeLife magazine

I've known Rodney and Selma Wilson for more than fourteen years. I've had the privilege of relating to them from several different angles. I met them when I became student pastor at First Baptist Church, Smyrna, where they and their two daughters, Jennifer and Natalie, were members. I had the privilege of becoming their pastor in 1998 at the same church. Then, a few years ago, Rodney joined my staff as Minister of Marriage and Family Enrichment. But the greatest privilege over the last fourteen years has been simply being their friend.

So I've seen firsthand how the principles they write about in *The Parent Adventure* play out in real life. I know for a fact that they don't just offer some theory that sounds good and sells books, but provide practical advice for real-life stuff in a real-life world. I know reading this material will help you be a better parent, and I highly suggest you recommend it to every parent and soon-to-be parent in your circle of influence. Giving people the tools to become better parents is one of the greatest gifts you can ever give. Thanks, Rodney and Selma, for helping me be a better parent. I love you both dearly.

Pat Hood
Senior Pastor
First Baptist Church
Smyrna, Tennessee

Parenting in today's world is more difficult than ever. Rodney and Selma Wilson have done their homework and written a book that includes solid research and practical ideas on how to parent from a biblical perspective. I highly recommend it to parents and to church leaders who want to equip their children to make a positive difference in the world.

Gary D. Chapman
Author of *The Five Love Languages*

Today's parents need biblical solutions to the challenges they face. *The Parent Adventure* equips parents and churches with biblical tools to impact children for Christ. Rodney and Selma capture the excitement of parenting . . . as well as the uncertainty that often accompanies navigating the journey. Parents will find Rodney and Selma's writing to be practical, encouraging, and grace-filled. Supported by LifeWay Research, churches will find these action plans to be the best practices for impacting children and their families for Christ. A must read for parents and church staff!

William Summey, Editor in Chief
ParentLife magazine

Motherhood has been shocking! I can't believe that after only two days real live professionals have allowed me to leave the hospital without a manual to keep me in line! With two small boys and another on the way, I'm continually amazed by the details, demands, and delights of parenting. Thankfully Rodney and Selma have heard our concerns and have pried open the pages of God's Handbook to give us the direction we desire and so desperately need. This page-turner is a "must read" for the fledgling and seasoned parent alike. It's stirring message for us and for the church of Jesus Christ will challenge and change the way we impact the next generation. Prepare to be blessed.

Priscilla Shirer
Bible teacher and author

THE
PARENT
ADVENTURE

THE
PARENT
ADVENTURE

PREPARING YOUR CHILDREN FOR A LIFETIME WITH GOD

RODNEY & SELMA WILSON
& SCOTT McCONNELL

PUBLISHING GROUP

Nashville, Tennessee

Dedication

From Rodney and Selma:

To our parents—Roy and Juanita Rymer and J. B. and Eudy Wilson: thanks for loving God, loving each other, loving us, and loving the church. The security of that love gave us wings to fly!

To our children—Natalie, Jennifer, and David: thanks for giving us the joy of experiencing "the parent adventure." We are better people because you are in our lives. What fun we are having watching you run after God and experience your own adventures with Him!

From Scott:

To Mom and Dad, whose unwavering love for God fueled your genuine interest in building relationships with my sister, Kim, and me. That's the way God intended families to work!

To Debbie, Madison, and Max, who know how much I have to learn about parenting. You are what's fun, what matters, and what I pray will last in my life.

Contents

Acknowledgments

We are amazed and humbled by the many gifted people who have worked with us on this project. First, to the LifeWay Church Resources team who had the vision and gave the challenge to help parents: Bill Craig, Mary Katharine Hunt, Scott Stevens, and Jeff Pratt. To Thomas Walters and the rest of the outstanding team at B&H Publishing Group and Judi Hayes who did a great job capturing this message for all parents. (Editing the voices of multiple authors and research takes great patience.) Thank you for not giving up on us or this message! A special thanks to Ron Sellers. We never regret working with you on a project! To LifeWay Research for giving us a much clearer view of the state of parenting today.

We are grateful to Pat Hood, senior pastor, First Baptist Church, Smyrna, Tennessee: your vision for having a marriage and family enrichment ministry at our church provided us the laboratory to test many of these parenting ideas. We are also grateful to Elaine Farmer and Ruth Meyer, dear friends and fellow staff members at FBC Smyrna, who shared with us their expertise on the developmental states of preschoolers and children.

A special thanks goes to our daughter, Jennifer McCaman, for going on this journey with us, using her amazing talents as a writer and editor in her own right, to make our message stronger and clearer (and for the many times she sat down and said, "That is not going in the book!"). Thanks to Jennifer and Natalie for making sure that all we remembered in our own parenting adventure was indeed true and accurate!

Also, a special thanks to Ivey Beckman, editor in chief of *HomeLife* magazine. Thanks for your friendship over the years, the personal investment you have given to our ministry, and for pushing us to be better writers than we could ever have been without your coaching and tenacity to make the words on a page sing.

Most of all we thank God for the abundant, extraordinary life He has given us through Jesus Christ. Every day is indeed an adventure as we experience the wonder of being children of God! For His grace and mercy that are fresh every morning. For the security we live in daily that our future is solid as we run the race to pursue Christ until the day we begin the ultimate adventure of eternity with Him!

We pray above all else that all who read this work would know Christ fully and experience this abundant, beyond-common life that is available for all of us.

Preface

What adventures have you had in your lifetime? The dictionary says that an *adventure* is "an exciting or remarkable experience or undertaking involving unknown risks." Parenting definitely fits that definition! That's certainly been the case for all three of us who worked together on this book.

When Bill Craig of LifeWay Church Resources' Leadership and Adult Publishing talked with us (Rodney and Selma) about writing this book, we began to discuss our own experiences in the parenting adventure and our thirty years of marriage and family ministry. We knew what that journey had been for us, but we wondered about other parents' experiences. Our parenting adventure had been influenced by our own families and especially by our relationship with Jesus Christ. We wondered about the influences that had helped to shape other parenting experiences. That's where Scott McConnell and LifeWay Research's partnership entered the picture.

LifeWay Research acted quickly to launch an extensive survey of parents across the United States. Because the research was carefully balanced demographically and included a sample size of twelve hundred parents, the results are dependable.

We also wanted to know what churches were doing to help parents and families, so through LifeWay networks we've found some ministry leaders who shared their stories with us.

All of that comes together to make this book unique. In Part I you'll find our story (Rodney and Selma) about our parenting adventures and some important steps we took in our parenting that made a difference with our children and with our own fulfillment as parents. In Part II you'll learn what churches are doing to make this adventure a church and family partnership. And from LifeWay Research you'll gain a clearer picture of the state of American parenting today.

Whether you're thinking about becoming a parent, you're already a parent at any stage, or you are a ministry leader with children, teenagers, or adults (parents), we wrote this book with you in mind.

Join us on the parenting adventure!

Part I

The Parent Challenge

Parenting can be both fulfilling and frustrating. Parents find great joy in their children, but they also want to improve their parenting skills, to do their best in raising their children. But where do they turn? The Internet? Their own personal experience? The advice of friends and family? How about the Bible?

The purpose of this first section is not simply to add another voice in the advice column. Rather it is to point parents to God's Word as the eternal, infallible source for truth in parenting and to offer six chapters of clear principles all parents can apply in their own parenting adventures.

Chapter 1

The Adventure Begins

> *Love the* LORD *your God with all your heart,*
> *with all your soul, and with all your strength.*
> *These words that I am giving you today are to*
> *be in your heart. Repeat them to your children.*
>
> —DEUTERONOMY 6:5–7

Twenty-seven hours. That's how long we were in labor before Jenny was born. Twenty-seven hours—that's tough on a dad. (I guess Selma did some of the work too.) The doctor placed her in our hands, and we were forever changed. She was our daughter, a part of us. We laughed and cried all at the same time. Fellow moms and dads understand that nothing could have prepared us for the moment we realized we were officially parents. It was as if time stood still.

Within the next twenty-four hours, I (Rodney) was captivated by the reality that I was a dad. Future responsibilities weighed on my heart. How could I protect her from the world? Clearly I would need to build a wall around our house to keep the boys out! No guy would ever be good enough for my girl.

Before Jenny was born, Selma and I read everything we could find on parenting, raising a newborn, starting a family, and more. We talked to friends and worked in the church nursery. We quickly learned the truth: nothing can fully prepare anyone to be a parent.

Now, after launching our own children from the home and spending more than twenty years ministering to families—caring for newborns, guiding preadolescents, raising teenagers, and sending young adults into the world—only one word captures the whole experience: *adventure*. Why adventure? Adventure is both dangerous and exciting. Of all that you and I will accomplish in this life (accepting Christ as Savior), one of the greatest blessings, joys, and adventures is being a parent.

A Gift from God

Like all great adventures, the parenting journey comes with pressure, stress, and exhaustion. For many, parenting is an incredibly intimidating concept. It can be tempting to hold your breath and (1) hope that your children are healthy when they're born and (2) pray that they don't give you as much trouble as the horror stories you have heard. Some people looking on from the outside might view the whole connection between parents and kids like a roll of the dice that determines how parents randomly get their kids. In fact, some parents may sometimes wonder if that's not exactly what happened to them!

In reality, chance has no part in your parenting adventure. God chose to give you the kids you have, and He does not make mistakes. We can find peace knowing that God is ultimately the

Creator and Giver of life. He created you, and He created your child! We are indeed wonderfully made. No accidents. No mistakes. Designed by our God for purpose and meaning in life.

Here is how the psalmist put it:

Oh yes, you shaped me first inside, then out;
you formed me in my mother's womb.

I thank you, High God—you're breathtaking!
Body and soul, I am marvelously made!
I worship in adoration—what a creation!

You know me inside and out,
you know every bone in my body;

You know exactly how I was made, bit by bit,
how I was sculpted from nothing into something.

Like an open book, you watched me grow from conception
    to birth;
all the stages of my life were spread out before you,

The days of my life all prepared
before I'd even lived one day. (Ps. 139:13–16 *The Message*)

In the New Testament, Paul wrote, "By Him, everything was created, in heaven and on earth, . . . all things have been created through Him and for Him. He is before all things, and by Him all things hold together" (Col. 1:16–17).

All about Him

If God created you, loves you, makes the plans for your family, you can find rest in Him. You can even enjoy the danger and excitement of parenting. Why? Because it's not about you. It's not even about your child. Actually, this parenting journey is all about God. Our purpose is to connect our children to Him. "Blessed be the God and Father of our Lord Jesus Christ, who has blessed us with every spiritual blessing in the heavens, in Christ; for He chose us in Him before the foundation of the world, to be holy and blameless in His sight. In love He predestined us to be adopted through Jesus Christ for Himself, according to His favor and will, to the praise of His glorious grace that He favored us with in the Beloved" (Eph. 1:3–6).

Throughout this study we want to show you how to create an environment for children to know God, to own their own faith, and to spend their life making God known. We will focus on parenting as a gift from God, a gift that ultimately centers on Him. You have been given the opportunity to touch the future. Through your child you can influence, encourage, and bless the next generation. With all of the unpredictability of any great adventure, parenting is an amazing gift from God.

LifeWay Research shows that by far the most common place for getting parenting advice was one's own experiences growing up,

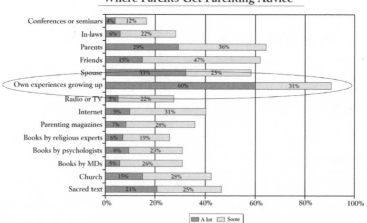

Figure 1. Where Parents Get Parenting Advice

> A heart connection is the pipeline that connects the hearts of the parent and child. Through that pipeline spiritual impact flows from one generation to the next. Parents who keep that heart connection warm and strong usually see visible evidence that their faith and values are passing to their children.
>
> —Richard Ross, *Parenting with Kingdom Purpose*

followed by parents, friends, and spouse. Just 21 percent said they get a lot of advice from a sacred text (e.g., the Bible).

The fact that you've picked up this book indicates that you have some level of interest in improving your parenting skills or, if you are a church leader, in equipping parents to improve their parenting skills. This study will give you some tools for this great adventure.

God and Parents

God probably gets special joy from parents because we must cling to Him desperately. If, as a parent, you've ever stepped back and thought, *I really have no idea what I'm doing,* you are certainly not alone. That's where God wants us because that's when we have to depend on Him. Nothing spurs us to pray like our children. After all, it's always wise to consult directly with the manufacturer of your "products."

When we rely on our own strength, we become like Peter walking on the water. Shifting his focus off of Jesus and admiring what he was doing, he began to sink like a rock. I once heard a pastor friend say that when we are out on that limb with no way to make it on our own, that is right where God wants us to be; that is where He can do His best work.

Parenting places us out on that limb. Thankfully God doesn't leave us to fend for ourselves out there. He assures us in His Word of His willingness to lead in our lives if we let Him. In John 10:10, for example, Jesus tells us that He came to give us a full, meaningful, beyond-common life. He said, "I have come that they may have life and have it in abundance."

> When American parents were asked about their familiarity with what the Bible says about parenting, only 14 percent felt very familiar with what the Bible says about parenting. Among parents with evangelical beliefs, the number is better but still only 52 percent.
>
> —LifeWay Research

Sometimes those persistent, iron-strong three-year-olds or teenagers with tongues of steel can come close to convincing parents that we are exempt from John 10:10. Understand that God doesn't call a John 10:10 time-out for parents of adolescents. He is not laughing and thinking, *Maybe when they get those rowdy kids out of the house, then they can have a great life.* The abundant life applies to our lives right where we are. Right *when* we are. Right in the middle and throughout whatever passage of life we are triumphing over or suffering through, including parenting kids of various ages and with unique personalities.

News flash: Parenting isn't for the faint of heart. Nor is the perfect parenting experience going to be handed to you. God never promised that any part of life would be easy or struggle free. Even in the middle of challenges, we can experience the promises of God's Word, His love, and His desire for us to have a fulfilling and overflowing life. If you are a Christ follower, John 10:10 will always apply to you. We must choose daily to live that abundant life. It is never forced on us. This book will help you see the need, and show you how to involve God in the great adventure of parenting.

Passing the Baton

When I (Rodney) was in high school (a while ago), I ran the 4x100 relay for our track team. Each member of the team carried the baton, ran one hundred yards with it, then passed it to the next team member. One year we were heavily favored to win the gold in the state meet. We were invincible (kind of like the *Titanic* was invincible!).

We could taste victory; all we had to do was qualify for the finals in heats run earlier in the day. This was cake. Easy for the fastest team in the state. I ran my one-hundred-yard leg, passed the baton to my teammate, and was putting on my warm-ups when I heard the most unusual sound. It was a collective sigh from the stands. Then those who ran against me kept saying how sorry they were for our school. As it turned out, our third and fourth runners dropped the baton during the exchange. The baton had not been properly passed, and our season was over just like that.

We parents have a responsibility to pass our "faith baton" on to the next generation. We must do our part to prepare our kids for their own unique adventure with God.

> Perhaps you are wondering if you are up to the task. Parenting is difficult enough without someone telling you that your primary responsibility is to instill in your children a passion for the kingdom. I have great news for you. You are not alone in this ministry. You have the resources of the Holy Spirit to enable you.
>
> —Ken Hemphill, *Parenting with Kingdom Purpose*

Passing on our faith is consistent with biblical examples. Abraham passed on his faith to Isaac, and Isaac passed on his faith to Jacob. Jacob passed on his faith to his twelve children, including Joseph. Jacob's children formed the tribes that later settled in the Promised Land. This came after Moses led the Hebrew people out of captivity in Egypt, and Joshua later led God's people into the promised land.

When the Hebrew people gathered on the Promised-Land side of the Jordan River, Joshua used a concrete illustration to help everyone remember God's protection and the fulfillment of His promise. He instructed a man from each of the twelve tribes to bring a stone from the river to create a memorial. Then he said, "When your children ask their fathers in the future, 'What is the meaning of these stones?' you should tell your children, 'Israel crossed the Jordan on dry ground'" (Josh. 4:21–22). Joshua instructed the people to tell their children what God had done.

Much later in his life Joshua led the people to renew their covenant with God and to recommit themselves to following only the one true God. He said, "Choose for yourselves today the one you will worship. . . . As for me and my family, we will worship the Lord" (Josh. 24:15).

The same is true today. Parents are called by God to pass on their faith to their children. How fast our track team ran didn't matter because we dropped the baton. As a parent, how much money you make, what car you drive, how much education you receive, your corporate position, your 401K, stock portfolio, and your handicap at the club do not matter. If you fail to teach your kids about God and His plans for their lives, you are running in vain.

The Best for My Kid

All parents want good things for their children. Of course we want them to succeed in life. If you ask parents what they want for their children, you can expect most parents to put some items like these on their list:

- Straight As
- College education
- College scholarship
- Healthy friendships
- Financial stability
- Common sense
- Favor with teachers
- Proficient reader
- Above average intelligence
- Strong work ethic
- Stable job
- Valedictorian
- Strong athlete
- Accomplished musician
- Racing after God
- Serving others
- Spiritual leader
- Faithful husband/wife
- Great parent
- Active in the church

Guess what? God wants the best for them too: "What father among you if his son asks for a fish, will give him a snake instead of a fish? Or if he asks for an egg, will give him a scorpion? If you then, who are evil, know how to give good gifts to your children, how much more will the heavenly Father give the Holy Spirit to those who ask Him?" (Luke 11:11–13).

Above everything else, however, we must give our children the truth of God. God's plans for our children will far exceed even the best of plans we make for them. God's Word is clear on our responsibility as parents. It is our job to "pass the baton" of faith to our children.

> In the end, the negative aspects of being a parent—the loss of intimacy, the expense, the total lack of free time, the incredible burden of responsibility, the constant nagging fear of having done the wrong thing, et cetera—are more than outweighed by the positive aspects, such as never again lacking for primitive drawings to attach to your refrigerator with magnets.
>
> —Humorist Dave Barry in *Dave Barry's Guide to Life*

Parenting Requires . . .

The parent adventure requires one of your most precious resources—*your time*. Nothing and no one can substitute for the time required of you as a parent to invest in your children. You can't give this time to your church, pastor, youth minister, grand-parents, friends, Christian school, or anyone else. All of these friends, relatives, teachers, and leaders can help you; but the prin-ciple job is yours. Time given to your child says: "I love you, period. Not because of what you do but because of who you are. I am for you. I believe in you. You matter to me." The parent adventure is about creating an environment that requires time for you to intro-duce your kids to God.

One biblical concept of parenting comes from an unlikely source. John 4 tells the story of the Samaritan woman at the well. Jesus talks with her, and she comes to believe that He is truly the Messiah. She puts her trust in Him and then goes back to her town and tells everyone there that she has found the Messiah.

Here's the cool part. In verse 42 the townspeople make this incredible statement to this woman. They tell her, "We no longer believe because of what you said, for we have heard for ourselves and know that this really is the Savior of the world."

Our role, like the Samaritan woman's, is to tell others about Jesus. When we, as parents, tell our kids about the saving grace of

> Making the decision to have a child is momentous.
> It is to decide forever to have your heart
> go walking around outside your body.
>
> —Elizabeth Stone

Jesus Christ, we pass along the baton of our faith. We ultimately want our kids to react like the townspeople: "Mom, Dad, I no longer believe because of what you have told me. You told me about Christ and modeled Him for me, but now I have heard/seen/experienced Christ for myself; and I know that He really is the Savior of the world." This is passing the baton.

The Parent Cathedral

Three workers labored on a stone wall. Someone walked up to them and asked each of them what they were doing. The first answered, "I am laying block." The second replied, "I am building a wall." But the third man proudly responded, "I am constructing a cathedral!"

Same question. Same wall. Same job. Entirely different perspectives on what they were trying to accomplish. One had a much bigger picture in mind.

In parenting we are doing much more than simply raising kids. We are touching the future. We are preparing our children for a lifetime adventure with God. We are impacting *their* children by how we parent them. We are not merely laying parenting blocks. We are constructing cathedrals!

This "cathedral-like construction" of a kid into an adult can look intimidating at times, but it can be done, and *you can do it!* With God all things are possible (see Matt. 19:26). And with Him parenting doesn't have to be a matter of survival. This can be one of the most exhilarating adventures of your life.

Will you take the challenge? Can you imagine what the next generation could be like, the difference they could make in the world, if parents who are missional Christians were to take seriously learning the truths from God's Word and passing on those truths to their children?

Adventure Road Map

This book will help you find practical ways to pass the baton of faith by creating a home environment where your children can learn about God through the day-to-day stuff of life. As parents, we want the formula. Many parents think, *Give me the five things to do that will guarantee this parenting thing will be a success. I want the simple, condensed version that promises if I do the formula my child will always be safe and have a happy, successful life.* It's not that simple, but research confirms the importance of the role of parents.

Research in the fields of psychology and sociology point to the critical role parents play in the life of their children. Here are a few examples:

- "Only 13 percent of teens surveyed said they trusted information from the Internet a great deal, compared to the 83 percent who trusted information from their parents a great deal."[1]
- "Nothing is more likely to produce a happy, well-adjusted child than a loving family."[2]
- MTV Research found that youth are happiest when they're with their family.[3]

Research clearly shows that parents play a significant role in our children's future, but research can't promise or guarantee the

---

"'Safe?' said Mr. Beaver. . . . "Who said anything about safe? 'Course he isn't safe but he's good.
He's the King, I tell you.'"

—C. S. Lewis, *The Lion, the Witch and the Wardrobe*

outcome. However, we can be 100-percent confident in God and the eternal truths from His Word, the Bible!

God is the only guarantee, the only promise for all of life. No matter what the future holds, God knows the future. Preparing your child for life with God *is* the parent adventure.

Yes, following God is exciting, challenging, rewarding, and dangerous at times. Some of the danger in the parent adventure lies in the risk, the fact that we cannot control how our children respond to our leadership. Take the prodigal son story told by Jesus in Luke 15. Same dad, two sons. One stayed home and obeyed all the rules, and one just flat out rebelled against dad and took off to a far country and lived wildly. We never want our children to go into that "far country," rebelling against God and us. But the good news is this: God, our heavenly Father, is always working and waiting for us to come back to Him. The guarantee is that our God is even able to redeem the mistakes of our lives as parents and the mistakes of our children and use them for good.

> **His father saw him and was filled with compassion. He ran, threw his arms around his neck, and kissed him.**
> –Luke 15:20

Our job as parents is to teach our children the ways of God. We live on the promise that even if they do rebel against us or God, they will not depart from the truth of God!

Here is an overview of the areas we will cover in teaching our youth about the way they should go:

"Letting Go"—Learning the truth that your child belongs to God and you can parent every day through every stage of your child's life with a confident understanding that you are to let them go to experience their own adventure with God.

"**A Yes Home**"—Creating a place where your children can grow, learn, create, and experience the joy and wonder of life while learning about a God who says yes.

"**Let's Talk**"—Sharing all of life together as family and learning to share openly the experiences of life lay the foundation for children to talk to God.

"**Pain Happens**"—Teaching your child that pain is real, both for us as parents and for our children, but God is always with us in and through the pain doing a work in our lives.

"**Celebrate**"—Building a home that looks for the blessings of God and regularly celebrates God's work in the lives of parents and children as an act of worship to God.

Throughout each of these chapters we'll take a look at the findings of LifeWay Research to touch base with what parents are saying and how church leaders can help.

Let the adventure begin!

The Prayer Focus

Each of our sessions together will end in a prayer. We will offer one as a sample, but we encourage you to end each chapter you read with a personal prayer. Paul's prayer to the Ephesians is a great prayer to pray as we start this parenting adventure together:

I pray that the God of our Lord Jesus Christ, the glorious Father, would give you a spirit of wisdom and revelation in the knowledge of Him. I pray that the eyes of your heart may be enlightened so you may know what is the hope of His calling, what are the glorious riches of His inheritance among the saints, and what is the immeasurable greatness of His power to us who believe, according to the working of His vast strength. Amen. (Eph. 1:17–19)

Parent Adventures

Are you ready to go on this adventure with us? At this point in each session we will have some specific actions you can do together with your kid(s).

1. Look together at photographs or videos of the early years of your child's life. Fix a special meal or picnic in the living room floor as a time of celebration for the gift of being a parent. Let your children know how thankful you are that God has allowed you to be their parent.

2. Tell your children that you are reading this book so you can be a better parent. If they are old enough, ask them to pray for you during this study.

3. Share one Scripture verse from this study with your children, letting them know what God's Word says about parenting. Look through this chapter for ideas.

QUESTIONS FOR DISCUSSION

1. Recall when you first held your child. What emotions did you experience?

2. What were your biggest concerns as a new parent?

3. How does knowing that God created you and your child affect your view of parenting?

Chapter 2

Letting Go

This is why a man leaves his father and mother.

—GENESIS 2:24

Jennifer and I laughed all the way to school that morning.
It was her first day of kindergarten, and I don't have to tell
you which one of us was more nervous (definitely Dad).
Maybe that's because she was my oldest or maybe because neither
of us knew how the departure from each other would go. So we
laughed.

In the parking lot I prayed a brief prayer that God would protect her from "everything" until Mom picked her up at 12:30 p.m.
I walked her down the hall until we found the classroom door.
The rest was a scene straight out of Hollywood. The music faded,
and the lights lowered. Jennifer's happy-go-lucky mood suddenly

grew somber as she looked up at me and simply said, "Good-bye, Daddy."

I smiled, kissed her good-bye, and somehow found my way to the car before I cried my way to work. I spent my entire thirty-minute commute pondering the enormity of her words.

Indeed it was good-bye. Good-bye to one chapter of parenting and hello to another.

Why Is Letting Go So Hard?

Jennifer's five-year-old wisdom made me realize that many more good-byes awaited us throughout this parenting adventure. My mind raced through elementary school, past the preteen and middle-school stages. I saw her standing in a cap and gown, graduating high school and moving away to college. Then marriage? I practically held my grandchildren before I got to work.

As I pondered the end of several stages of her life, one reality gripped me most: one day parenting my kids would end. One day

> I had rather you should remain hundreds of miles distant from us and have God nigh to you by His Spirit than to have you always with us and live at a distance from God.
>
> —Jonathan Edwards to his daughter, Mary from *The Works of Jonathan Edwards, Vol. 1*

I would no longer be the provider, protector, teacher, disciplinarian, and all-around dominant figure in my daughters' lives. The responsibility of raising Jennifer and Natalie was temporary. And this changed everything.

That night I shared my experience with Selma. We began to pray and to rethink our entire parenting philosophy. Instead of dreading the good-byes around every corner, we would use them to fuel our parenting. We determined to start with the end in mind, and the clock was ticking. Immediately we would begin letting go a little each day to prepare our children to stand on their own when the time came for them to be completely independent.

We hit our knees that night, recognizing our total dependence on God. We acknowledged that our girls belong to God who created them and knew the plans He had for them. We were able to get up off our knees, confident in Him and more at peace with the unknown.

The majority of parents are fearful about what their children will face in the world as adults, including one-third who feel this strongly.

Do Parents Feel Fearful about the Future?

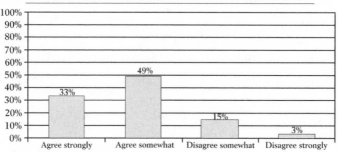

Figure 1. Do Parents Feel Fearful about the Future?

Just over half of all parents look forward to the day their kids grow up with excitement that they'll be ready to face the world. A third of parents are fearful of letting go, of what will happen when their kids "leave the nest." They think of this day with fear and worry over whether they'll be ready; 15 percent said that simply thinking about their future empty nest is too painful.

The Letting-Go Leap

The idea of releasing your children into a cold and cruel world can be pretty scary. After all, we pour ourselves into our offspring for nearly two decades. We give spiritually, emotionally, and physically, not to mention financially. We sacrifice so they can have what we didn't. We put our social lives and sometimes our careers on hold to invest in their development. We are twenty-four-hour counselors, peacemakers, lawyers, doctors, teachers, tellers, philosophers, clowns, coaches, mentors, maids, chauffeurs, and more.

Then one day all of that ceases. Your role in parenting changes; the job where you never really grasped what you were getting into in the first place is finished.

For a while it can seem like a small identity crisis. The momentary pain of letting go, however, is unquestionably necessary for both you and your child. Watching your child soar toward adulthood, confident and secure in Christ, will bring incredible celebration.

You can rejoice over their leaving the nest. Your children are ready for an independent adventure with God. You will take on a different role in their lives, a significant role but not the direct hands-on role you once had. Don't forget, God has many more post-kid-raising adventures for you before your life on this earth ends. (Maybe even grandparenting!)

Fast-Forward

Jen is married now, embracing her own adventures with her husband. The kindergarten episode seems so long ago. Natalie, our younger daughter, is in her senior year of college, dreaming big dreams for her future with God. What about your kids? It may be next year or twenty years from now, but your children will grow up and (hopefully) leave home to experience everything God has in store for them. The parenting adventure allows us to get them ready for the day of "letting go."

On that long-ago morning I thought about what I wanted for my daughter as I envisioned the years passing by. Maybe on the list below you will see some things you want for your own children.

- Strong believer in Christ
- Responsible and trustworthy
- Spirit of humility
- Serves those in need
- Financially independent
- Able to stand up for himself/herself
- Bold in sharing their faith
- Spiritually grounded
- Submissive to authority
- Grateful
- Positive, optimistic
- Loves the Bible
- Seeks wise counsel
- Able to distinguish truth from propaganda
- Servant leader
- Takes initiative, self-motivated
- Faithfully involved in a church
- Able to admit mistakes and accept responsibility
- Patriotic adult
- Loving servant
- Independent leader
- Discerning in relationships

As parents whose children have said good-bye, we glance back now and can see how God has taught us to let our children go.

Mom's First Let-Go

Rodney planned a special celebration for our tenth wedding anniversary. For several years he had taken college students on mission trips to New York City. This time he wanted just the two of us to go together. Natalie was eighteen months old at the time, and I had never left her. When Rodney let me know that the trip was all set, I had six weeks to get ready to let my girls go. I cried, I prayed, I even fussed (to myself) at Rodney's insensitivity for making me leave them for three whole nights. It seems like a small thing now, but it was huge then. Thankfully, we had dear friends—Steve and Carolyn. I trusted them with our girls, but I still had growing pains to face.

The big day of "letting go" came and went. I noticed that I was already developing some "hold on too tight" patterns as a young mother, so the break was good for all of us. The girls survived (more like thrived) while Rodney and I had a wonderful time celebrating our marriage, ministry, and even our children.

I laugh now even as I write this. Leaving my girls for a few days was only the beginning. Here are some other milestones of "letting go":

- first sleepover at a friend's house
- first overnight school trip
- first boy-girl event
- first youth missions trip
- first time they drive without you
- first day of their first job
- first overseas missions trip

Letting Jesus Go

Even Joseph and Mary had some issues with letting Jesus grow up to be the chosen One that His Father wanted Him to be:

The next day [Mary and Joseph] found him in the Temple seated among the teachers, listening to them and asking questions. The teachers were all quite taken with him, impressed with the sharpness of his answers. But his parents were not impressed; they were upset and hurt.

His mother said, "Young man, why have you done this to us? Your father and I have been half out of our minds looking for you."

He said, "Why were you looking for me? Didn't you know that I had to be here, dealing with the things of my Father?" But they had no idea what he was talking about. (Luke 2:46–50 *The Message*)

Whose Kid Is It, Anyway?

When we parent with the end in mind, our perspective changes. We realize that we don't own our kids. They never really belonged to us; they were always God's. We begin to recognize our role as caretakers, guiding them through childhood, phase by phase, good-bye after good-bye, change after change to a point of independence. Eventually, our children must say good-bye to us in order to embrace fully God's ultimate plan for their lives. Even in the beginning, God started the family with the parents letting go: "This is why a man leaves his father and mother ["Good-bye, Mom and Dad"] and bonds with his wife, and they become one flesh" (Gen. 2:24).

We essentially work ourselves out of a parenting job. Our spirit should be like John the Baptist's attitude toward Christ ("He must increase, but I must decrease," John 3:30). Likewise, our kids must increase (in their independence), and we must decrease (by letting them go.)

If children are only with their parents for a while, then whose kids are they really? They belong to God, who created them and holds the plans for their lives (see Jer. 29:11). He promised that He will never leave them or forsake them (see Heb. 13:5).

If God is the "Ultimate Owner" of our children, then what is our role? We are simply, but significantly, their managers, getting them ready for their own adventure with God that they will live out long after we are gone.

Biblical Parents Who Let Go

The Bible contains several examples of parents who recognized that they did not own their kids. While their techniques are unique by today's standards, these parents clearly acknowledged God as the ultimate "parent" of their children.

From Fear to Freedom (Exodus 2). As a Hebrew slave, one mother lived in fear for her newborn. After Pharaoh ordered the death of all baby boys, she concealed Moses in her house for three months. When she could hide him no longer, she chose a basket, coated it with tar and pitch, and placed her baby inside. As she set her son afloat upon the Nile River, Moses' mom relinquished her role as protector and provider, trusting God to save him. He certainly did.

> It takes courage to let our children go, but we are trustees and stewards and have to hand them back to life—to God.
>
> —Psychiatrist Alfred Torrie

Back to God (1 Samuel 1). In ancient Jewish culture, Hebrew women longed to bear children. After years of praying for a child, Hannah went to the temple. She poured her heart out to God with such fervor that the priest thought she was drunk. Hannah promised God that if she had a child, she would give him back to God. Eventually God allowed Hannah to have a son, Samuel. She kept her word and presented him to God at the temple when Samuel was still very young. "I prayed for this boy, and since the LORD gave me what I asked Him for, I now give the boy to the LORD. For as long as he lives, he is given to the Lord" (vv. 27–28).

Obedient Mother-in-law (Ruth 1). Naomi knew what it was

like to lose everything. Within a few years her husband and two sons died, leaving her with no immediate family. Instead of clinging desperately to her daughters-in-law, she released them, commanding them to return to their homeland to be blessed with new husbands. One woman left, but Ruth refused. To Naomi's astonishment Ruth vowed never to leave her mother-in-law. God honored Naomi's decision to "let go" by giving her Ruth and, eventually, an amazing new "son."

Letting go is an act of love, the greatest foundation for parenting. We let go because it is best for our child (maybe not always best for us, or so it seems). Letting go requires a strong faith and trust in God who loves our children even more than we do.

Strength in Stewardship

Perhaps you're familiar with the concept of tithing (giving 10 percent of our income to God). Though we specifically designate this portion, God holds us accountable for how we spend all of our money. It all belongs to Him, and we are simply the stewards of what He sends our way.

Similarly, we are the stewards of the precious gifts of our children. God has entrusted them to our care. He will hold us accountable for how we spend our time as stewards, raising the kids He has loaned to us. Part of that stewardship involves preparing them for their own adventure with God separate from Mom and Dad.

How to Let Go

Even after you let go, your relationship with your children continues of course. You simply begin to relate to them differently. Your role in your child's life will change. It has to change, or you'll have a twenty-five-year-old asking for your approval to take his wife on a weekend getaway. Your permission! At twenty-five?

Start by letting go today. Trust me. You want your son to get to the point where he can decide about an overnighter with his wife without you.

Think back to the ideal adult characteristics listed earlier. Your child will not transform into an independent, godly adult overnight. Letting go starts right now. No matter their age, your children can learn independence at each stage.

These suggestions will get you in the "letting go" frame of mind.

> When we leave our child in nursery school for the first time, it won't just be our child's feelings about separation that we will have to cope with, but our own feelings as well—from our present and from our past, parents are extra vulnerable to new tremors from old earthquakes.
>
> —Fred Rogers from *Family Wisdom* by Susan Ginsberg

Infants–6 months

• Pray over them. Have a specific time of commitment to God in raising your child to know Him.

• Leave them with others such as family, friends, and the church nursery workers. Don't sneak out. (This causes anxiety and clingy behavior next time.) Instead, say good-bye and reassure them you'll be back. Of course, when you leave your children, you need to be responsible about the people you trust to care for them (this is true at every stage), but leave them you must.

Preschoolers

• Give them choices. Allow them to start thinking on their own and making decisions. For example: "Apple juice or milk?" "*Cat in the Hat* or nursery rhymes?" "Sandals or tennis shoes?"

ELIZABETH'S PATH

Now I'm not one of those "yard of the month" guys, I can assure you. But I do like my yard to look good, and I take a certain amount of pride when the edges are straight and the grass looks nice and full. So last year when my daughter began to take the same path to her car across our front yard day after day and a definable, noticeable path developed through the flower bed and yard, well, let's just say I didn't like it a whole bunch.

"Could you walk around on the sidewalk? Don't you see the trail you are making there?" I didn't fuss a lot about it, but every once in a while I'd mention it to her but to no avail.

But the other morning I noticed something. Now that she's completed her senior year and headed for college in a few weeks, her routine has changed enough that the path has grown back over, and you can't see it at all anymore. Suddenly this thought hit me right out of the blue: She will never make that path again. And I'd give anything in the world for another year with Elizabeth's path through my front yard.

I thought about that a minute and was reminded of one of my favorite verses in the Bible: "A man's heart plans his way, but the LORD determines his steps" (Prov. 16:9).

Elizabeth will make more paths in her life. They just won't be in my front yard. The next one will be at Union University. And she has further plans in her heart to make paths through elementary classrooms someday as a teacher and, then as God directs, in the lives of a husband and a family. I will closely watch every one of them develop and will love seeing my little girl make her mark on the world.

But I also know and take great comfort in the fact that God is the One directing her steps. So from now on, when I look across my front yard, I'll remember her path and think about the mark she has made in my life. And this father will ask God to guide every step as she blazes new trails and impacts a world for His glory.

And I will revel with joy as I follow Elizabeth's path.

—Mike Harland, from *Seven Words of Worship*

• Let them make mistakes and learn from the consequences. For example, warn your child that she is about to drop something, then let her drop it. If she is about to spill a glass of milk, tell her, then let it spill. Don't warn her, then fix the problem. Let her clean up her own messes.

• Give age-appropriate responsibilities: pick up your toys, get your blanket, and carry your bag. Preschoolers can also help set the table and feed the dog. Don't major on perfection, but value their independence in the completion of the task. Let them do it "their way."

• Prepare yourself. Honestly, you're the one who will experience the greatest separation anxiety, not your child. Sometime before preschool, plan a night out—just parents. Leave your child with a trusted babysitter.

> Give your child the gift of a strong and healthy marriage. Leave your child to focus on your marriage!

Elementary-Age Children

• Encourage children to speak to adults. For example, don't let them depend on whispering in your ear when they want you to ask an adult for them. Say, "You can ask them." This will help them interact with others and speak for themselves. This will equip them to function when you're not around.

• Allow them to attend a field trip without you.
• Let them ride the school bus home. (My kid? Yes, *your* kid!)
• Have them order their own meal at a restaurant.

Preadolescence

• Allow them to sleep over at a friend's house (if you know the parents).

> Doing your child's homework is a bit like
> believing that they can get into shape by
> watching someone else exercise.
>
> —Psychologist Laurence Kutner in *Parent and Child*

• Provide only necessary assistance with schoolwork. (Don't do their projects for them.)

• Allow them to disagree with you respectfully and form their own ideas.

• Challenge them to take risks like auditioning for the school play or trying out for the team. If they don't make it, pour on the encouragement and teach them again about God's plan for their lives. (See chapter 4, "Pain Happens.")

High School Students

• Allow them to get a job.

• Teach basic survival skills like balancing a checkbook, changing a tire, paying bills, cutting coupons.

• Allow them to go on a church mission trip without you.

• Let them plan and coordinate supervised parties at your house for holidays or birthdays. Put them in charge of invitations, decorations, food, and activities. Make them work within a budget.

• Encourage them to serve somewhere in the church (children's ministry, media, choir, teaching, bookstore, greeter).

College Students

• Help them break away financially. Establish a budget, and expect your child to work (at least during the summers).

• Allow your child to make her own dating choices.

• Give freedom over your child's schedule. You don't need to know where he is 24-7.

- Allow college-age children to fight their own battles with professors, friends, and other relationships. Give advice and support, but let them make the final call.
- Allow your child to attend a church of her choosing.
- Let them choose their own major, job, career path. Identify their gifts, but never squash their dreams.

Letting go helps develop children at each stage of development for that day when you launch them from your home to begin their own independent adventure with God. Author of *Nurturing the Leader within Your Child*, Dr. Tim Elmore explores seven "Marks of Maturity" signs that you can watch for in your children that indicate they are maturing intellectually, emotionally, and spiritually.

1. They are able to keep long-term commitments.
2. They are unshaken by flattery or criticism.
3. They possess a spirit of humility.
4. Their decisions are based on character not feelings.
5. They express gratitude consistently.
6. They prioritize others before themselves.
7. They seek wisdom before acting.[1]

Teaching Your Child Spiritual Truth As You Go

Each phase of "letting go" is an opportunity to live out our responsibility and calling as parents. Every parenting decision we make from birth to young adulthood prepares our children for their own adventure with God. "Love the LORD your God with all your heart, with all your soul, and with all your strength. These words that I am giving you today are to be in your heart. Repeat them to your children. Talk about them when you sit in your house and when you walk along the road, when you lie down and when you get up" (Deut. 6:5–7).

Every time you let go in little and big ways, you remind your children of who created them and who holds the plans for their lives. You emphasize the truth of God and His Word. In the everyday ordinary and extraordinary stuff of life, you have the privilege and responsibility of pointing your children to God.

- God created them.—"Your works are wonderful, and I know this very well" (Ps. 139:13–15).
- God loves them.—"Nor any other created thing will have the power to separate us from the love of God" (Rom. 8:38–39).
- God has a plan for them.—"For I know the plans I have for you" (Jer. 29:11).
- God has gifted them in unique ways.—"You do not lack any spiritual gift" (1 Cor. 1:7; 7:7).

At every stage of your child's life, look for ways to let go and teach the truth of God at the same time.

The Prayer Focus

Father, it is so scary to let go of my children. I want to hold on tight and protect them from the world. Give me courage to let go so they will ultimately learn to put their trust in You. Give me wisdom in the day-to-day adventure of parenting to teach my children about You. Help me, Father, to let go a little more today so they can be more fully ready for all that You have planned for them. Most of all, let my children see You in me so they will come to put their faith in You. Amen.

Parent Adventures

1. What three actions can you take this week to begin "letting go"?
2. What can you tell your child about how God is working in your life as you let them go?
3. What can you share with your child from God's Word? Pick at least one Scripture verse to share with them this week. (Hint: looking back through this chapter for some ideas is allowed!)

QUESTIONS FOR DISCUSSION

---

1. Describe a time when you expect to, or have already, "let go." What challenges will you/did you experience during this "good-bye" stage?
2. What "letting go" experiences have you already had with your child? What lessons did your child learn? What lessons did you learn?
3. Since God holds the plans for your child's future, how does this impact your parenting?
4. How has your church helped you during these letting-go moments? How could the church help you?

Chapter 3

A Yes Home

> *For every one of God's promises is "Yes" in Him.*
>
> —2 CORINTHIANS 1:20

The Wilsons' family nights usually went like this: we'd eat dinner, play a game or two, watch our favorite shows, then hit the sack. Easy enough until our older daughter Jennifer, then six, proposed a wacky idea: *Why couldn't we eat dinner on the living room floor?*

It was a simple request, clearly something neither mom nor dad had ever imagined. We looked at each other; then Selma responded with two words that began to change our parenting experience: "Why not?"

From that moment family night was transformed in the Wilson home. The weekly spreading of the checkered tablecloth on the living room floor marked the beginning of family night and family fun.

Our living room (with Dad's help) magically transformed into exciting destinations. We entered the jungle by moving a few plants around. We constructed campsites (our favorite) by throwing sheets and blankets over furniture. (Caution: These adventures can be messy.) From pizza in the jungle to roasting marshmallows with toothpicks over a candle, family night became the perfect place for our children to be children. In addition to laughter and imagination, family night also allowed Mom and Dad to teach some of life's greatest lessons.

Pizza in the middle of the jungle? Roasting marshmallows on a toothpick over a candle? *Why not?* (But somehow Mom always managed to "escape" to the bedroom at some point in the night while Dad ended up on the floor in the tent protecting the girls from a potential bear or tiger!)

Friday nights became a protected tradition in our family for many years. It began with a question sparked by the imagination of a little girl and a mom and dad saying yes to her new idea.

Burst of Creativity

At some point every parent is amazed at how God weaves creativity into the DNA of a child. Genesis tells us that God has made us in His image (1:26), which guarantees that within each of us is the amazing potential for creativity!

If your children are anything like ours, they hatch some pretty imaginative schemes. Have you noticed that children are full of so many questions? "Daddy, why does a bug crawl?" "Mom, can we touch the stars?" Creating a yes home early on builds an environment for the more challenging questions you want your children to ask as they move through life.

Kids need direction and discipline for sure. Along with

boundaries, however, children crave a place to exercise physically, intellectually, emotionally, and spiritually. A yes home with clearly established boundaries gives them room to stretch, run, and grow with your guidance and instruction within reach. As parents we have the responsibility to foster that creativity and give it room to grow. We call this a "yes home."

The Many Kinds of Yes

Being open to ideas from your children, sometimes going on their kind of vacation, solving problems their way, eating family night dinner where they want to eat it create a yes home. Saying yes to your children, when you can, builds a healthy environment in your home, your family, and your attitude as a parent. It sets the tone for healthy relationships founded on respect and value for each family member.

Every parent can find hundreds of ways to build a yes home, even when your children are young. Your yes can be as simple as a three-year-old's wanting to play with plastic blocks in the bathtub. Your yeses can begin as Mom thinks, *The blocks have always been in the bedroom. I've never thought about using them in the tub. But why not? I'm not going to say no when I can say yes.* Then to her child she says, "Yes, let's give *them* a bath first, then they can join you in the tub."

That same kid, at fifteen, may ask you if the sleepover can be at your house. Once again, if there are no major problems and the daughter agrees to her part in getting ready, then why not?

Our friends and parents of three started a yes home in the kitchen with weekly special dinners. One of their kids asked, "Why can't *we* make dinner sometimes to help Mom?" That started it. For years afterward one night each week a different family member would prepare dinner. (The younger ones had Mom's oversight of course.)

Saying yes to a child's cooking creation was challenging. (No doubt *eating* some of those creations was challenging for sure!) However, each week everyone celebrated the contribution to the family dinner. The child's creativity plus the parents' yes developed a new weekly ritual that quickly became a tradition that lasted for years.

Childhood and Beyond

God has planted certain gifts within our children. We have the privilege of fueling those gifts with a yes home environment. By saying yes to your children when you can, you value their creativity, raise their confidence, and encourage them to explore the passions God has placed in them for the plans He has for their lives. Often this means "coloring outside the box." A yes home sets the environment for connecting your child to God.

> Your child must learn to appreciate his or her God-given uniqueness. Nothing will have a greater impact on your child's total development than a clear understanding of his or her unique design by sovereign God.
>
> —Ken Hemphill, *Parenting with Kingdom Purpose*

Now fast-forward a few years: How would a yes environment impact your grownup child? Maybe he will continue thinking outside the box in other areas of his life. Perhaps he will find a cure for a major disease or develop new systems in education, business, technology, or on the mission field. Maybe she will have the courage to step out in faith and say yes to God's call on her life. A yes attitude could help your child fight mediocrity and strive for God's best throughout their lives.

In our survey, when asked to describe their home environment, most of the responses were positive. Few were negative. A majority said their home is supportive, positive, encouraging, active, joyful, and relaxed. This was reinforced in part by their descriptions of what their home environment is not.

Despite the majority of parents viewing their home positively, a sizable minority couldn't describe their home with those words and many more do not know how to encourage such a home environment.

Yes Is a Decision

When your child asks you if he can do something off-the-wall, the default response is often no. No is safe. It is status quo. And no is a lot easier to say. There's no risk involved. No wondering what others would think if they knew the whole family played outside in the rain one day. No messes to clean up.

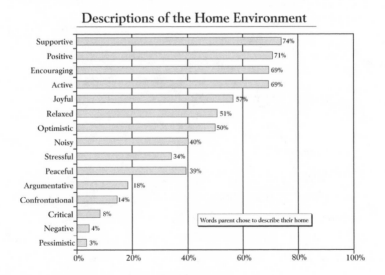

Figure 1. Descriptions of the Home Environment

The yes response has to be intentional, and it starts before the question ever comes. Parents need to *predetermine* that they will at least consider their kids' ideas and not immediately write them off as childish and immature. To change your default setting, turn off the instant no and ponder your child's request. Even when the answer needs to be no, your child can feel valued that her idea was respectfully considered.

Part of a yes home means sometimes saying no. Along with hundreds of yeses, parents also clearly need to define some nos. Children want and need boundaries. Occasional nos create security. Our heavenly Father understands this perfectly. God gave us the Ten Commandments in the context of hundreds of yes-driven promises (we'll look at some of these later in this session). He gave Adam one "no tree" in the garden compared to numerous "yes trees." Both the promises and the boundaries were crystal clear. "And the LORD God commanded the man, 'You are free to eat from any tree of the garden, but you must not eat from the tree of the knowledge of good and evil, for on the day you eat from it, you will certainly die'" (Gen. 2:16–17).

Payoffs of Saying Yes

A yes home can develop your child spiritually, emotionally, and physically.

Yes Empowers

The three-year-old who gets to put her toys in the bathtub because *she* thought of it has been encouraged to think outside the (toy) box. Her confidence in her own creativity will grow. Over the years this confidence will begin to unleash the abilities and passions that God has placed in your child. When children are ready to embrace Christ and own their own faith, they will be ready to unleash these gifts to impact the world with the truth of Jesus Christ.

Yes Esteems

Children feel valued and respected when Mom and Dad take time to listen to them. In a yes home their voice is not only heard, but it is also expected! The yes mind-set says to the child: "We want your input. Your ideas are important to us. Part of your role is to share your suggestions, your opinions, and your viewpoint with our family. When we can, we are going to say yes to your idea. But regardless, your voice is needed and welcomed." This builds confidence and courage in children so that in the future they will be able to speak up about critical issues of faith and justice.

> When I think of my father, the memories that bubble to the surface are not policy or politics. They are of the man who opened a child's imagination.
>
> —Patti Davis, daughter of Ronald Reagan, from *All About Dad* by Dahlia Porter and Gabriel Cerrantes

Yes Encourages

From ages six to sixteen, a kid's confidence is going to skyrocket when parents place that kind of value on their child. With each yes you are ultimately getting them ready to say yes to God. Each yes is an opportunity for you to encourage them with the truth of God.

Navigating the Nos

In the proper context of a yes home, the nos actually become easier. Here is a classic way to deliver a no to your child:

I (Rodney) had just turned sixteen. I had my driver's license a few months when winter came with its sleet and ice. As I was getting ready for a big date, the storm arrived. My dad entered my room with a rare no on his mind. I will never forget that talk. (I've drawn from it many times in my own parenting.) He told me that he trusted my driving, but he didn't trust others in the icy weather.

Then he played the dad trump card. He said, "You know I don't tell you no very often, but tonight . . . no." He had me. Yes, I was disappointed, but *how* he said I couldn't go and the fact that he told me no so seldom gave me no ammunition to disagree with his decision. Even in the context of this particular no, this was a yes home in action. All of Dad's and Mom's previous yeses impacted my response to this rare no.

The Necessary No

Building a yes home means you clearly need to establish some nos. Your children want boundaries. They want to know you love them enough to say no. Just as God gives us some clear nos as His children, the parent adventure requires nos.

For example, respect was an absolute in our home. From our earliest years of parenting to the launching of the girls, we insisted that family members show respect to one another in word and deed. We created a no-tolerance mind-set toward disrespect. Disagreement and even anger were permitted within the boundaries of respect at all times. Disrespect was corrected firmly and immediately and always in the context of teaching our girls about God and His Word.

Here are some other nonnegotiables in the Wilson family:

- No, you do not get a pass on helping out around the house. Every member of the family has daily responsibilities.
- No, you can't play at your friend's house unless I meet the parents.

- No, you can't stay up late and sleep through church on Sunday.

Sometimes our kids' wacky ideas push our limits. Not every idea your kid dreams up should automatically be accepted. The key is balance. Save your nos for the most important times, and say yes when you can. Sometimes those wacky ideas can begin some awesome family traditions.

Pictures of Yes

On the other side of the coin, here are some possible yes questions your kids may ask you:

Preschooler: "Mom, can I play dress up with some of your old clothes?" "Dad, will you teach me how to dig up worms?"

Elementary Age: "Can we get up in the middle of the night and watch for shooting stars?"

Preadolescence: "Can I invite my friends over for a campout?"

High Schooler: "Can I go on the student mission trip to Brazil?"

College: "Can I study abroad?"

Leaving a "Yes" Legacy

My (Selma's) mom was dying of cancer. She sat on our living room couch. Her hair was gone from the chemo treatments; she was hooked up to an oxygen tank; her body was weak, but her mind was sharp. Our girls were seven and nine, and they were playing around the house. I had finished a load of laundry and was sitting with her folding the clothes. Mom spoke some powerful words to me that day, words of affirmation but also words of challenge. "Selma, always remember that your girls are more important than so much of life. More important than a clean house, perfect meals, and even those clean clothes. Spend more time with them, playing, reading, and just being. You and Rodney are good parents, but don't ever lose sight of the important things of life."

I received so many gifts and blessings from my godly mom and dad, but that day is marked forever in my memory. In Mom's own way she was saying, "Build a yes home."

Biblical Models of Yes

"As God is faithful, our message to you is not 'Yes and no.' For the Son of God, Jesus Christ, who was preached among you by us—by me and Silvanus and Timothy—did not become 'Yes and no'; on the contrary, 'Yes' has come about in Him. For every one of God's promises is 'Yes' in Him. Therefore the 'Amen' is also through Him for God's glory through us" (2 Cor. 1:18–20).

Ultimately, a yes home is important because you want your child to know the God of yes! Through Jesus Christ we can live a yes life.

- Yes, you can ask Me for wisdom (see James 1:5).
- Yes, I will keep on loving you forever (see Rom. 8:37–39).
- Yes, you can do all things through Me (see Phil. 4:13).
- Yes, I will finish what I started in you (see 1 Thess. 5:24; Phil. 1:6).
- Yes, I will forgive you (see Eph. 1:7; 1 John 1:9).
- Yes, you can have a full and meaningful life (see John 10:10).
- Yes, I will protect you (see Pss. 32:7; 18:10).
- Yes, you can approach Me with confidence (see 1 John 5:14–15; James 5:16).
- Yes, I have a plan for you (Jer. 29:11).
- Yes, I can work everything in your life for good (see Rom. 8:28).

- Yes, My followers, you will spend eternity in heaven with me (see John 14:1–4).
- Yes, you are beyond condemnation (see Rom. 8:1).
- Yes, you are a member of His kingdom (see Col. 1:13).
- Yes, you have been adopted (see Rom. 8:15).
- Yes, you have access to God at any moment (see Eph. 2:18).
- Yes, you will never be abandoned (see Heb. 13:5).
- Yes, you have an imperishable inheritance (see 1 Pet. 1:4).

And so many more yeses! God said yes to us by loving us so much He gave His only Son to die for us so that we can live a yes relationship with Him!

Building a yes home gets your children ready to say yes to God. In every yes experience you have as a family, teach them a yes truth about God. The Bible offers many examples in Scripture of people who said yes to God.

Mary said yes. "'I am the Lord's slave,' said Mary, 'May it be done to me according to your word'" (Luke 1:38).

Esther said yes. "I will go to the king even if it is against the law. If I perish, I perish" (Esther 4:16).

Saul/Paul said yes. "Immediately he began proclaiming Jesus in the synagogues: 'He is the Son of God'" (Acts 9:20).

David said yes. "Then David said, 'The LORD who rescued me from the paw of the lion and the paw of the bear will rescue me from the hand of the Philistine'" (1 Sam. 17:37).

Abraham said yes. "So Abram went, as the LORD had told him, . . . Abram was 75 years old when he left Haran" (Gen. 12:4).

Teaching Spiritual Truth as You Go

Each yes and each no in our parenting adventure give us an opportunity to teach our children about God and His work in the world and in our lives.

Let's go back to the foundational verse for our parenting adventure: "Love the LORD your God with all your heart, with all your soul, and with all your strength. These words that I am giving you today are to be in your heart. Repeat them to your children. Talk about them when you sit in your house and when you walk along the road, when you lie down and when you get up" (Deut. 6:5–7).

Throughout each phase of parenting, you will have many opportunities to say yes and many opportunities to say no. Remember that each yes and each no prepares your child for life with God. Ask God to give you wisdom to know when to say yes and when to say no.

Yes Home Warning

Parents, we must warn you: *Yes homes are people magnets!* If you begin to build a yes home, not only will you impact your children, but you'll also draw others from your church, school, neighborhood, and community. People want to be in a yes home. As each member of your family learns to say yes to God's work in their lives, those who walk through your door, sit at your table, grill out in your back yard, and sleep over in living room tents will also experience it.

Your child's friends will want to come to your house to hang out. Your house will get even messier, and you might be inconvenienced, but you'll have limitless opportunities to teach many children the truth of God.

We vividly remember the little-girl sleepovers and overnight teenage parties. Many children and teenagers passed through the doors of our home. Food was always involved as well as lots of laughter, music, games, and frequent opportunities to share the truth of God and His plans for life.

Get ready. God wants to use your family and your yes home to impact the world for Him.

The Prayer Focus

Father, thank You for the blessing of being a parent. Give me courage to say yes to You in my own life. Help me to build a yes home so my children will learn more about who You are and be ready to say yes to You. Give me wisdom and courage to be strong with my nos and the wisdom to know where to set "no" boundaries for my children. Thank You for saying no to me and giving me boundaries to live by, and thank You for the yeses You speak to me every day. Help my children see You in me. Amen.

Parent Adventures

1. What can you do this week to build a yes home?
2. What can you tell your child about how you have said yes or no to God in your own life?
3. What are the three most important nos or rules for your children at this stage of parenting? Write them out. Be clear. Don't ground them for three years, but do establish consequences.
4. How can you communicate God's yeses and nos to your child? Pick at least one Scripture verse to share with them this week (look through this chapter for some ideas).

QUESTIONS FOR DISCUSSION

1. What questions are your children asking? What are some yes answers you can give?
2. Write six yes statements. What crazy, wacky, outside-the-box creations can you say yes to based on your child's developmental stage?

3. Which one of these yes truths have you experienced recently? How has it impacted your life?

4. Is God currently asking you to do something, and you know you need to say yes? What is holding you back? What can you learn from men and women in Scripture who said yes to God?

Chapter 4

Let's Talk

Life and death are in the power of the tongue.

—PROVERBS 18:21

I think you love Jennifer more than me." Natalie was four and had called a family conference. We all gathered in the living room after she boldly made this statement. We can't remember everything that was said, but this "talk system" allowed Natalie to express herself openly. We laugh about it now, but we were able to deal with something that could have become a critical issue. What if Natalie was unable to express her view? We're glad we had a safe place for her to share.

We began having family conferences in our home when the girls were in preschool. The rules were simple: *Anyone could call a family conference for any reason.* We held family conferences about taking family vacations, sharing household chores, getting a pet, negotiating allowance, doing missions projects, making Christmas plans, addressing critical family decisions, and many other topics. Calling a family conference became an informal way for the members of our family to learn to express their views on the stuff of life in a way that all of us could learn to listen and to help one another. It also became a key family forum for prayer as we took the ordinary stuff of life to an extraordinary God for guidance and help.

Time to Talk

Talking is essential in the parent adventure God has planned. His Word is clear: parents are responsible for passing on the baton of faith to our children. This responsibility belongs to no one else, and it cannot be relegated to anyone else—not the church, the pastor, the student pastor, the Christian school, or anyone else. (We know many of you reading this book may have the responsibility for parenting because the natural parents are not able to fulfill their role for whatever reason. Blessings to you! God will honor and bless you for standing in the gap.)

LifeWay Research discovered the median amount of time parents spend with their kids each day is three hours; in other words, half spend more than three hours and half spend less.

The younger the oldest child is, the more time is spent with the children.

Time spent with children drops substantially as the child gets older.

Blended families spend less time with their children.

Psalm 78 gives us a clear picture of our responsibility to take the time to talk to our children:

My people, hear my instruction;
listen to what I say.
I will declare wise sayings;
I will speak mysteries from the past—
things we have heard and known
and that our fathers have passed down to us.
We must not hide them from their children,
but must tell a future generation
the praises of the LORD,
His might, and the wonderful works
He has performed. . . .
He commanded our fathers
to teach to their children
so that a future generation—
children yet to be born—might know.
They were to rise and tell their children
so that they might put their confidence in God
and not forget God's works,
but keep His commandments. (vv. 1–7)

Talk Is a Command

Let's look again at our key verse for *The Parent Adventure:* "Love the LORD your God with all your heart, with all your soul, and with all your strength. These words that I am giving you today are to be in your heart. Repeat them to your children. *Talk* about them when you sit in your house and when you walk along the road, when you lie down and when you get up" (Deut. 6:5–7, emphasis added).

Talking to our kids is required if we are going to obey God's command to us! This chapter is about helping you build strong communication between you and your child—all for the purpose of connecting them to God.

Fear Not "the Talk"

Perry McGuire, an attorney in Douglasville, Georgia, is married to Lauren. They have four children. Perry teaches engaged/ young married couples at their church in Douglasville. Here's his first-person account of having "the talk" with his son:

> I recently took my twelve-year-old son on a trip to discuss the birds and bees. We set off to the beach. I had armed myself with several books and tapes to watch and discuss. I thought this would get me off the hook from having "the talk." While the resources were great, they didn't go into the detail I wanted my son to know. So, we took long walks along the beach. I would ask him to explain the tapes we watched. I am glad I did. There were some things, that to hear him explain, it was clear that he was clueless about, and that could get him in trouble in the world.
>
> Of course, these walks resulted in a couple of other things. First, it was very hard not to spontaneously explode into gut-busting laughter at some of the things he would say. I made my mind picture us in a serious clinical setting. I let him know that every question was a very good question, and when he gave an incorrect interpretation, I let him know that I could understand how he could come to his conclusion, but I would then proceed to give him the correct explanation.
>
> The second result was my newfound ability to lecture to the sea. On some topics I simply could not look at him, and I realized that he had the same problem because he would be looking down at the sand. But I was determined to tell him all the things that I wish I had known, so I toughed it out (wiping the perspiration from my forehead as needed).
>
> We also had some great recreational time, an important component in creating a positive experience for both of

us. We played a couple rounds of putt-putt and watched a couple of guy movies.

In the end, what hit me like a rock was that inside this big boy (and I do mean big—he is almost as tall and strong as I am) is still a boy—naïve, curious, and a little scared of what his future holds. The greatest gift that I can give him is knowledge of the truth and security in knowing that he will not have to go it alone. His heavenly Father and his earthly father will stand shoulder to shoulder with him, and it will be his dad, not his friends or the media, who has his back.[1]

Set the Stage to Talk

Families commonly eat dinner, watch TV, play games or sports, and attend events and activities together. In fact, a majority do these together weekly. These times together are opportunities for families to put talk systems to work and to engage each other.

The right environment is critical for communication. The busyness of twenty-first-century family life may be the greatest challenge to talking with your child. We are not going to ask you to check out of the culture, to get rid of all your 24-7 technology toys, but we *are*

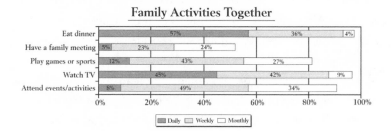

Figure 1. Family Activities Together

going to zero in on some steps you can take in the middle of life.[2] These steps will help you create an environment that prompts conversations with your child. The subjects will change, but each conversation is an opportunity for you to teach your child about God.

No matter where you or your children are in the journey of life, you can practice these ideas. Most of these steps will take minutes, not hours or days, but they will begin to build a relationship between you and your child that will last a lifetime, a relationship that will allow you to teach them about God.

Family Conferences

Anyone in the family can call a conference, anytime, for any reason. Everyone in the family is part of the time together. Keep it informal, but make it a total family experience. No topics are off-limits. Start early and build this into your home. The safe topics will allow for the more serious talks that will happen over time.

Bedtime

Pay close attention to the minutes before your child goes to sleep. At the end of a day, we are tired, our defenses are down, and these moments together can be a powerful time of sharing. Turn off the noises of life—computers, iPods, DVDs, cell phones, TV (a lot to unplug!)—and really spend a few minutes together as a family. Make the end of the day a time of laughter and fun as everyone gets ready for bed. (When our girls were little, they rode "Daddy horsy" off to bed.) Predictability and routine build confidence and trust, creating intimate levels of talk. This is also a great time for prayer. We're more likely to share from our hearts at night. What an opportunity for you to teach the truth of God and the power of talking to Him!

Bedtime provides great reading time for the family too. Books are great adventures for all members of the family. I (Rodney) spent years of daddy-daughter times reading books to the girls. We went through the Chronicles of Narnia and many other great works of literature. Books can also spark great life discussions.

Mornings

Like your family, ours contains those who love mornings and those who would prefer to skip them entirely. Rodney and Natalie wake up ready to talk, sing, and happily greet the world. Selma and Jen prefer joyful morning people to keep their distance.

Whatever your family makeup is, work on mornings. The beginning of the day sets the tone for the rest of the day for every member of the family. Minutes count in families and life. We highly recommend that you start by getting up a few minutes before everyone else in the family and just spending some quiet time with God. Even a few minutes of focused time will make all the difference as the chaos of the day starts full speed ahead!

Get creative on specific things each family member can do to make the mornings more positive. From getting clothes and school things ready the night before to giving "slow to rise" children fifteen extra minutes to get their motor going, work on it.

Focus hard on the last five minutes before you separate. Make sure your child starts the day with a blessing from you.

Reentry

If members of the family have been apart during the day, emphasize the "back together" moments. Stop, focus, touch, make eye contact—share together the stories of the day.

One of my (Selma) most powerful memories as a child was the "reentry" time with my mom. When I got off the school bus every day for as long as I can remember, my mom was waiting for me. Most of the time she would have a snack waiting at home, and we would sit in the kitchen and talk. Mom wanted to know about my day. Sometimes we would spend just a few minutes, but sometimes

I would have a lot to say. These times built a strong bond of security for me.

Mealtimes

A great deal of research has been done on the impact of eating family meals together and their value to children: increased nutritional value, high performance in school, developing a high degree of belonging, and overall fewer behavioral problems.[3] LifeWay Research indicated that 57 percent of families say they daily eat together as a family. Let mealtime be a focused time for investing in your children.

All of this is true, but one of the greatest values of mealtimes together is creating a focused time for families to talk and share life together.

Maybe eating every meal together is impossible for your family, but call that family conference and agree on how many meals you can have together. Take turns preparing the food (meal preparation is a great life-teaching experience!), mix up where and how you have the meal (picnic in the backyard, formal meal with good china and candles, blanket in the living room floor, etc.).

Family Adventures

From living room picnics, to backyard campouts, to weeklong vacations together, every family adventure is an opportunity to share life together and talk, preparing your child for life with God. These focused times help you build "talk systems" into your family life. Before you earn the right to talk to your kids about the big stuff (relationships, spiritual growth, sex, etc.), you need to

> "Talk systems" are focused times you build into your family to share, listen, and learn from one another.

show you are interested in talking about the seemingly trivial things (clothes, sports, who sits by whom at lunch).

Showing interest in their world at every stage of their childhood creates the environment for you to connect them to God and the great adventure He has planned just for them. From bugs to boys, from kiddie pools to swim team, from playing dress up to a formal social function, from finger painting to modern art, a healthy talk system can allow you to connect their passions, abilities, and interests to God and the plans He has for their lives.

Can You Hear Me Now?

What would you say if I asked you to name a parent's most vital communication tool? As you teach your children and prepare them for life with God, you will talk to them, but even more critical is that you listen. You need to listen to your children with your eyes as well as with your ears.

We love to teach and counsel. One of the reasons is because of the immediate feedback we get on what we've just shared. The same is true for parents when communicating with children. If we will take a moment to notice, it becomes evident whether our point was clear. As that brilliant philosopher, Yogi Berra would say, "You can observe a lot by just watching."

For example, in our time of counseling couples, we can tell within the first few minutes with them if the husband feels respected and if the wife feels loved. We don't learn that from the words they say but just through the nonverbal cues they give each other. Respect for a husband and love for a wife are key indicators of how their marriage is doing.

The same is true in parenting. Once you've shared a thought, a word of wisdom, answered a question, or explained why the level of discipline was given, then just watch. Most kids will immediately let you know if you're making sense. But you've got to watch and listen for those nonverbals.

Kids often "scream" nonverbal messages through facial expressions, body language, eye contact, and voice tone. In order for parents really to hear their children, they must put all the communication pieces together, the nonverbals as well as the words that are actually being said and the tone used to express them. Some parents tend to talk *to* their kids and not *with* them, resulting in a fruitless one-way conversation, oblivious to nonverbals.

> **Keep talking—learn the love languages of everyone in your family and then express love in ways they understand.**
>
> **—Author Gary Chapman**

Stop the lecture long enough to see if you have a listening audience or just a body in front of you. There's a big difference. If you feel like you're talking to a brick wall, stop. Rephrase, ask questions, and get your child to respond.

If your child is not openly sharing through words, you'll want to pay even closer attention to what is being said through nonverbal cues. You may need to initiate the talk by saying things like:

"Son, you seem sad."

"I can tell you're really angry."

"I notice how happy you are when you . . ."

When our girls were preschoolers, we started saying to them, "Look at my nose." It was a fun, light way to get their attention. Some parents might say, "Look at me," or, "Look at my eyes." Often this technique is used to emphasize discipline and correction. We also used their undivided attention to bless them and teach them truths about God.

"Jennifer, we are so glad God let us be your parents."

"Natalie, God has a plan for your life."

> Listen, my son, to your father's instruction,
> and don't reject your mother's teaching, for they
> will be a garland of grace on your head and
> a gold chain around your neck.
>
> —Proverbs 1:8–9

"Jennifer, God has given you some amazing gifts and abilities."

"Natalie, we are proud of you for just being you."

The "look at my nose" technique goes both ways. You want your child to zero in when you make an important point. Likewise, you need to give your children your undivided attention when they're expressing themselves. You need to watch your children carefully to see if your words get through. Do they hear and receive your encouragement? Do they seem confused? Who would have thought healthy parent-child communication would involve a nasal exam?

As parents, we need to: (1) stay alert to communication opportunities; (2) become a student of our kids, learning the unique ways in which they ask for attention; and (3) pray that God will sensitize us to hear that call for attention when it comes. Responding to their "attention cry" can do wonders in developing communication.

Raising Your CQ (Communication Quotient)

One of my (Rodney's) initial goals in counseling is to get each person to open up, to share what's going on. People will not feel comfortable until they feel somewhat secure in the environment: the office setting, how I operate, and so forth.

When a husband and wife come in, for example, my sensitivity is higher toward the husband. I want him to know that I'm not going to "burn him" in front of his wife. As security builds, the wall

TEN POWER STATEMENTS PARENTS CAN SAY TO THEIR KIDS

1. Yes.
2. How can I pray for you?
3. Will you forgive me?
4. God has a plan for you!
5. We are excited that you are growing up (entering a new stage of life)!
6. I know it hurts.
7. You are more important to me than . . . (you fill in the blank—report cards, work, sports, etc.).
8. I am so glad you are in our family.
9. I love you too much to let you do that.
10. Try to be patient with me. I've never been the parent of a (10, 12, 14, 16) year-old before. (Caution: This only works with the firstborn!)

comes down, and he begins to reveal what's really on his mind with their marriage.

A secure foundation is essential for meaningful communication. I might confront a husband on an issue but not before I've built some "communication credibility" with him.

With your child, a similar foundation of security and trust needs to be established before honesty has a chance. We can't offer a secret formula that produces instant closeness. You can, however, foster "communication potential" by spending time with your kids, cultivating trust, and showing interest in your kids' lives. Building communication potential makes genuine conversation and closeness more likely.

Communication doesn't happen in a vacuum. If you want to have a meaningful relationship with your child, start to develop a pattern of security and trust. See how the following components build on one another.

- Good communication comes from two parties opening up.
- Opening up comes from trust.
- Trust comes from confidence in each other.
- Confidence comes from security.
- Security comes from an environment of safety, an atmosphere that says: "I am genuinely interested in you as a person, not to control you or to lay my agenda on you. Not to preach you a sermon. I am on your side. I believe in you and want the best for you."

Talking as You Go

These practices are better *shown* to your kids than *told* to them. Here are a couple of dad-daughter examples.

In her teens Jennifer and I would often get away for a tennis date. She played on her high school team, and it was a good excuse to "keep the old man in shape." Driving to and from the courts gave us some good talk time. Sometimes we would extend the date by catching a burger after the workout.

Once she was dating this guy who was, well, let's say he was a little short in character compared to the man she eventually married. (OK, he was a *lot* short of David, her eventual husband!) Our times together became the perfect vehicle to allow us to have those deeper conversations.

The interest and investment in one part of Jen's life (tennis) cultivated the security she needed to open up in more personal areas. In the end Jennifer made her own decision about "Mr. Character" (and she made a good one, too!). But I was able to share my opinions (convictions!) about him because she knew I cared about all of her life, not just whom she dated.

Natalie and I love to work complicated jigsaw puzzles. We will spend hours fitting pieces, laughing, philosophizing, talking Spanish (her more than me!), theologizing, and dreaming while looking for just the right one of three hundred pieces of sky. The whole time we work, we are building two foundations: one for the puzzle and one for communication. Sometimes we don't talk about anything significant. Yet even the most mundane conversation is building confidence and security in the relationship, allowing the more serious talks to happen down the road. Sometimes communication is spelled T–I–M–E.

Today Natalie is away at college, but our times together continue. Our weekly phone dates are on Monday nights—late, of course. (When else? She's in college, and besides, we are both night owls.) The first few minutes are always filled with sarcasm, a corny joke, or Dad's carrying the Spanish conversation as far as he can!

This date night has gone on for years, and I greatly cherish it. The "raising" of Jennifer and Natalie is over. They consult us only if they choose to now. But the time we've spent together lets them know they can still come to us with anything. The communication door is still open.

> The best inheritance a person can give to his children is a few minutes of his time each day.
>
> —Author O. A. Battista

Every conversation you have with your kid affects the next one. You are either building communication potential or tearing it down. For example, show interest in your kid's world. She knows that you do not know everything about her world of MySpace and texting. However, she *will* know you care about her. On the contrary, if you disrespect her thoughts and put her down, she'll doubt your sincerity, and your next conversation will be less meaningful.

Communication Levels

You will want to experience communication with your child on several levels. We learned most of these from marriage enrichment leaders David and Vera Mace, but they also apply to parenting.

Level 1: Small Talk

This is where most of us live. It is talk about the day-to-day stuff of life. You want a healthy dose of small talk in your family. Most of our communication will be at this level. How we handle the ordinary, everyday stuff of life sets the tone for reaching the extraordinary levels of communication you want with your children.

Example: You teach your child how to throw a ball, cast a fishing pole, or bake a cake—just stuff. But right in the middle of reviewing a ball-tossing technique, you have that moment when your child asks a question about life and you can say, "Look at my nose. God has a plan for your life." The beginning point of good communication and great adventures is small talk and lots of it.

Level 2: Sting Talk

This unhealthy communication style has a "stinger in its tail." It contains those little barbs of sarcasm and manipulation that can hurt deeply. Work to eliminate these from your family at all costs. They seem innocent enough, but over time they take on a toxic level of danger that shuts down healthy communication.

Paul wrote, "Fathers, do not exasperate your children, so they won't become discouraged" (Col. 3:21). Sarcasm and hateful talk are never productive.

Here are some examples of sting talk:

"If only you were more like your sister."
"You never do anything right."
"I wish you would just go away and leave me alone."
"Would you stop asking so many questions?"

"It figures. I didn't think you could."

Watch for these poisonous remarks in your home. When they happen (after all, we are all human), stop. Deal with them immediately. Say, "I'm sorry. I'm tired, but I shouldn't have said that." You can always recognize these statements because they "sting," and someone feels the pain.

Level 3: Search Talk

This level happens when you share your dreams and goals. Every great adventure has dreams. Where would you like to go? What would you like to be? What would you like to build? Where would you like to sing?

This type of communication is fun and allows every member of the family to stretch and grow. Every child needs to feel the freedom to dream. We as adults can learn much from the wonder of a child who is just being a child—the magic of pretending and adventure only a child can experience.

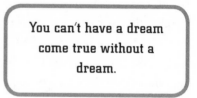

You can't have a dream come true without a dream.

Building search talk into your children at an early age will allow them to open their eyes and hearts to all that God wants to do in their lives as they move into adulthood. This type of conversation can help them discover their passions as they discover God's plans for their lives.

Jane Creswell is an executive coach who calls herself "a missionary to the corporate world." Whether talking with her children, working with a missionary, or coaching the top executive in a large corporation, she finds that asking questions helps people think through situations, evaluate answers, and find their own solutions—and they can do this in the safe context of talking with her and testing their answers. She frequently studies the probing questions Jesus asked. They are great models for parents to use.[4] Consider these:

- "If you love those who love you, what reward will you have? Don't even the tax collectors do the same?" (Matt. 5:46)
- "Can any of you add a single cubit to his height by worrying?" (Matt. 6:27)
- "Why do you look at the speck in your brother's eye but don't notice the log in your own eye?" (Matt. 7:3)
- "Why are you fearful, you of little faith?" (Matt. 8:26)
- "Who do people say that the Son of Man is?" (Matt. 16:13)
- "But you, . . . who do you say that I am?" (Matt. 16:15)
- "What will it benefit a man if he gains the whole world yet loses his life? Or what will a man give in exchange for his life?" (Matt. 16:26)

Asking questions and listening for answers is a great way to talk with your kids. You'll show them respect. You'll teach them to think and to listen. You'll encourage them to have confidence in themselves. It's a great way to talk with your children.

> Then Jesus said, "Leave the children alone, and don't try to keep them from coming to Me, because the kingdom of heaven is made up of people like this."
>
> —Matthew 19:14

Level 4: Straight Talk

The deepest level of communication is straight talk, the "feelings" level. This is where you share matters of the heart. One of the guidelines in our home was "feelings are not right or wrong; they just are." God has given us a full range of emotions to express life. In all great parenting adventures, both parents and children will experience a full range of feelings. As you build healthy talk into your home, you will find that sharing feelings is a powerful way to teach.

For example, anger is often a secondary emotion that can easily be misunderstood. When a child (or an adult) seems angry, our first response is to stop the anger. After all, it usually isn't a very pretty sight. "Jamie, you shouldn't be angry." "Caleb, go to your room until you get over your anger."

I (Rodney) was counseling a pastor whose teenage son was going through a rebellious period. Major tension had developed between father and son. The father expressed his anger, but at a deeper level he was hurting over his son's choices. I told him to share his hurt with his son. He said, "But Rodney, that's how I share my hurt—*through* my anger!"

Now, granted, letting the anger cool off so you can talk may take time. However, don't miss the "what is behind the anger" opportunity with your children, whether they are two or fifteen. Often you will discover "gold" as you gain insight into your child's expanding world. Many times you will uncover fear, hurt, insecurity, or uncertainty, or all of the above. What a relief uncovering the real issues can be to kids, letting them deal with some or all of those buried feelings.

A feelings level of communication is packed full of opportunities for you to teach your child. Let your home be a place where feelings can be openly expressed.

Preschool

"Daddy, I'm scared of the dark."
"Mommy, I love music."

Elementary Age

"Joey hurt me when he called me 'four eyes'."

"I really love my science class."

Middle School

"I'm so ugly."

"I'm so stupid."

"I think I like this boy in my gym class."

Adolescent

"I get so angry when you say that."

"I feel God is calling me to be a missionary."

College

"I'm afraid to go away to school."

"I'm excited about going away to school."

Level 5: Tough Talk

Parents, it is up to us to have the tough conversations with our children. Sometimes they mess up, and it's up to us to confront them with truth. It is part of preparing them for life with God.

Avoiding sting talk doesn't mean you avoid discipline. It means even in the middle of tension and disobedience, you will be firm yet strive to show Christ to your children while helping them learn from their mistakes.

"Son, I love you too much to let you do this."

"You've broken my trust, and you will need to build it back. Until then I am going to require more from you."

"Sin always has a consequence. I can't fix this one for you."

"You will not talk to your mother like that."

Lessons from the Bible

"When your children ask you, 'What does this ritual mean to you?' you are to reply, 'It is the Passover sacrifice to the LORD, for He passed over the houses of the Israelites in Egypt when He struck down the Egyptians and spared our homes.' So the people bowed down and worshiped" (Exod. 12:26–27).

This passage explores "the teachable moment" talk. We as parents need to: (1) live a godly lifestyle that will prompt questions from our children about the way in which we live, and (2) anticipate the questions, being prepared to answer our children—not with a sermon but with a well-thought-out response that will make sense to them, an answer on their level. When your children ask, be ready!

At a football game when a guy jumps off sides, what does the referee do? He doesn't get red-faced and begin screaming about the virtues of keeping the rule. He drops the flag and he steps off the penalty. In the same way, when your child messes up, don't break the peace of your home. Step off the penalty and do it consistently. Don't reason with the little guy. Discipline him.

—Author James Dobson

Here is a talk scenario in which a parent can start at one level and go deeper.

Watching TV has become so engrained in America's homes that it has virtually become the family's favorite pastime. How healthy a family's TV watching is depends on how TV is approached. We can all envision glassy-eyed viewers staring with jaw open, so mesmerized they don't even hear "Dinner's ready!" You may also be thinking how frequently the TV can "keep your child out of trouble" while you get some things done.

Think for a moment about the talk potential of TV. This only occurs when you have watched the same shows as your kids. Since 87 percent of families do this together each week, let's consider the opportunities.

> Sixteen percent rated the amount of time the whole family spends together as excellent, while most (65 percent) rated it either good or very good.
>
> —LifeWay Research

Watching the shows your kids enjoy with them builds trust and security in the same way you do by taking an interest in their hobbies. You can easily "talk as you go" as you watch most shows, but you must be intentional or you too will be glued to the TV.

As you intentionally engage in small talk during a show, look for opportunities for deeper "search talk." For example, when your son says something is "cool," ask him if he would like to try "that." When your daughter admires a lead character, ask her if she would like to have that character's job when she grows up.

Tough talk directed toward the TV characters or producers allows parents to teach children boundaries that the child herself

> Just 53 percent of families pray together once a month or more, and only 31 percent do any religious devotionals or studies together that often. Yet more than nine out of ten watch television together once a month or more.
>
> —LifeWay Research

has not crossed. For example, Scott noticed that a character on a show Madison was watching had given all his video games to someone else because his family had joined a cult. The show made light of this as the character left to go shave his head. Scott quickly asked Madison if she knew what a cult was. She responded by saying she wanted to know. Scott briefly explained that a cult is a group of people who believe things about Jesus Christ that are different from what the Bible tells us. He made clear that the TV character's family had made a bad choice. Madison would never have wanted to know what a cult was if it had not surfaced on TV. By taking advantage of the opportunity, Scott was able to give a biblical answer to an important question he didn't want just anyone providing.

Teaching Spiritual Truth as You Go

One of the most amazing experiences we have as children of God is to talk with Him and have Him speak to us. God has planned a "talk system" that is amazing. When we talk with God, He hears us and speaks to us through His Spirit living in us, through prayer, and through His Word.

> Don't worry about anything, but in everything, through prayer and petition with thanksgiving, let your requests be made known to God. (Phil. 4:6)

> Pray constantly. (1 Thess. 5:17)

> At daybreak, LORD, You hear my voice;
> At daybreak I plead my case to You and watch expectantly.
>   (Ps. 5:3)

> Listen, GOD! Please, pay attention!
> Can you make sense of these ramblings,
> my groans and cries?
> King-God, I need your help.

Every morning
you'll hear me at it again.
Every morning
I lay out the pieces of my life
on your altar. (Ps. 5:1–3 *The Message*)

Building a strong talk system with children helps them grow and develop honest and open communication with God, which is essential for life.

Family Activities Together

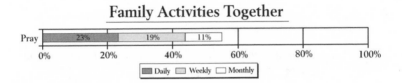

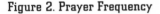

Figure 2. Prayer Frequency

Unfortunately only 53 percent of families pray together at least once a month. Only half of all parents are taking advantage of this opportunity to introduce their children to a relationship with God.

When you let your children hear and see you pray, you prepare them for life on their own. Real, honest, open prayer. Prayers of petition, prayers of thanksgiving, truly going to God with all the stuff of life, big and small. This should be as natural to us as talking to one another. God says to us, "Just talk to me." Talking to God gives us perspective on everything else in life!

The Prayer Focus

Father, thank You for allowing me to talk to You anytime and anywhere. I am staggered by the reality that I can even be in Your presence. Thank You for Jesus who makes it possible for us to talk. Oh Father, use me today to teach my children to talk to me but more importantly to talk to You. Again, I give them to You. Use me to get them ready for life with You. May they see You in me today. Amen.

Parent Adventures

1. What can you do this week with your child that says, "Let's talk"?
2. Are there any new "talk systems" you want to add to your family? (See ideas in this chapter.)
3. What can you share with your child about God's work in your life through prayer?
4. What verse can you share with your children this week that will teach them about the importance of talking to God? (See ideas in this chapter.)

QUESTIONS FOR DISCUSSION

1. What are some issues your family has recently talked about?
2. What are some current issues going on in your family that you need to talk about?
3. What does Scripture teach about talking to our kids? What are some of the things we need to be talking about with them?
4. What passions, abilities, and interests are you seeing in your child?

5. What are some "look at my nose" statements you can make to your child?

6. What do your children do when they want your attention?

7. What are some activities you can do with your child to create opportunities to talk?

8. Describe a time someone used "sting talk" to you? How did it impact you?

9. How can you encourage your kids to dream big dreams? What is a dream you have that you could share with your child?

10. What are some feelings you are seeing expressed in your children right now? If they aren't telling you how they feel, how could you begin to talk to them about what you are seeing?

11. Which level of communication does your family do well?

12. Which level do you need to work on?

13. What are your children seeing in your life that would cause them to ask questions about God?

Chapter 5

Pain Happens

Each day has enough trouble of its own.

—MATTHEW 6:34

ost of the Wilsons' craziest adventures happened in the Great Smoky Mountains, our family's vacation spot while the girls were growing up. Every summer we hiked trails, climbed rocks, picnicked, camped, and played miniature golf. Our favorite tradition, however, never escaped the itinerary: Cades Cove biking. Even before the girls could ride their own bikes, they loved to sit in the baby seats and ride along behind Selma and me. Biking through God's creation provided a peaceful, soothing family excursion—that is, until Jen started riding her own bike.

Sayonara, serenity.

She was six years old, and her feet barely touched the pedals. Still, we agreed Jennifer was old enough (we thought) to ride alone, and we assured her that all would be well. Unfortunately, we discovered that the steep hills, which challenge most adults, terrify small children.

Riding down one such hill with Natalie strapped in the seat behind me, I heard Selma scream. I turned around to see a horrified look on Jen's face. She had lost control of her bike and was now barreling down the hill, both legs straight out, eyes closed, and the pedals whirling faster and faster. She shot toward a nearby oak tree like a heat-seeking missile.

In that instant, I (Rodney) had a tenth of a second to decide which daughter I would "sacrifice." I could drop my bike, and Natalie by default, or I could watch Jen smash against a tree. I quickly released my bike and stepped over to snatch Jen off her runaway bike-train. Her velocity spun us around a full 360 degrees.

Meanwhile, Natalie, our four-year-old, minding her own business, enjoying the beauty of the mountains, suddenly collided with the gravel road. For some reason she started to cry. Thankfully, she only suffered a small scratch that I don't think she even noticed.

After a few moments the family settled down. Natalie stopped crying, and Jen got back on her bike. We rallied and continued the twelve-mile loop, spotting some deer and enjoying the peaceful scenery once again.

That night, reality sank in. I remembered feeling unnerved when I saw Jennifer's face. She was going to crash into that tree at a hundred miles per hour (it seemed), or Natalie was going to have a quick meeting with the road. Either way, pain stared my family in the face. I told everyone I was sorry for Nat's pain, but I didn't know what to do. Selma and Jennifer assured me I did the right thing as Jen could have gotten a concussion from the inevitable tree crash. It took her a little longer, but Natalie finally agreed. (Sometimes being a four-year-old is tough!)

Often when Selma and I recall that incident, I tend to go into guilt mode, somehow feeling that it was my fault. Her response is always, "Yes, Natalie was hurt but not as bad as Jennifer could have been. And besides, Rodney, *the adventure, the memory, is worth the pain.*"

We came to agree that pain would occasionally happen in our family. We also determined that pain and discomfort would not be the end of the world.

Our family has experienced more than a decade of mountain adventures. What if we decided to "avoid all pain" by staying home and never discovering the beauty of God's creation? I think of all the wonders we would have missed: the sunrises, the thrill of catching a fish, the awe of seeing a bear up a tree, the grace of deer running through the meadows, the wonder of waking up and finding yourself enveloped in the mist of clouds, the campfires, and the glow of kerosene lamps as we talked of life and God.

> **Parents are not irresponsible because their children experience pain. The irresponsibility comes when parents do not teach children the lessons found in the pain.**

Our adventures in God's creation almost always cost us some pain or occasional discomfort. For instance, on another Smokies trip, we climbed a huge river rock when I (Rodney) slipped and fell, injuring my hip. On one six-mile mountain hike, Natalie, who was seven, started crying, sat down, and said, "I just can't go on." She was exhausted, so we rallied around her and rested for about an hour. When we finally convinced her to continue, the campsite was just around the bend.

Years later, on another bike ride, Selma and I experienced the "pain" of getting older, especially when our teenage girls had to stop and wait for us at the top of every hill—a long way from rider seats!

The Parents' Problem with Pain

Whether enjoying a vacation adventure or experiencing regular, everyday life, parents will never prevent all pain. This is a challenge for parents because it's natural for us to want to protect our kids. Think about it. From the day babies are born, we want to keep our kids safe. Stairways get blocked, breakables go into storage, and everyone who wants to hold our baby must submit to an FBI background check.

We are the ones who fight for our children, and their safety ultimately falls on us. We naturally want to build a safety net—spiritually, emotionally, socially, and physically—so that nothing can hurt or scar our precious gifts. However, safety is not the greatest gift you can give your children. When taken to the extreme, the safety net hurts more than it helps.

> Sometimes life hurts. Sometimes life is not fair. You are not necessarily a bad parent when your kid has a painful experience.

No creature understands pain like the caterpillar. Trapped inside the cocoon, it must slowly and painfully build muscle by ripping through the cocoon wall. The child who comes along and opens the cocoon damages the butterfly by stunting its wings. The caterpillar gets instant relief, but it will never fly.

Ironically one of the greatest gifts you can give your kids is the ability to handle pain. You can help your children pray, struggle, and wrestle through the pain of life until one day they are strong enough to stand on their own—ready to fly. Instead of running away or fixing every problem, prepare your kids for life with God by teaching them spiritual truth in the middle of the pain.

Perspective in the Pain

When kids are young, it's hard for them to see beyond the pain. One skinned knee or finger burn and the world is over. In adolescence the pain is often caused by a broken heart or the mean MySpace post that shatters a kid's world. Parents can offer perspective and help kids see pain as an opportunity to grow.

I (Selma) got the call. Jennifer was crying hysterically on the other end of the line. Flashes of possible crises ran across my mind. "I didn't get the lead part in the play." Now, mind you, she got a part, just not the *lead* part, the one she had counted on and auditioned for. To top it off, one of her friends got the part instead of her. In Jennifer's adolescent world this ranked right up there as a major crisis! I could do nothing to stop her pain. I felt that helpless feeling all parents feel sometimes.

When your child hurts, you hurt, and soon I found myself crying right along with her (and wanting to call her obviously deaf music director). Instead, I called a dear friend to give me counsel. What does a mom do when she can't fix the pain? We hurt together as a family and listened to Jen talk about it for days (and days). Eventually, we were able to discuss key truths about life not always being fair and how God would use this to strengthen her trust in Him. The play went on, and she did great in her part. More importantly, she grew through the entire experience. God was shaping her.

The pain of life isn't fun to experience ourselves or to witness as it happens to our kids. Yet pain can provide many teachable moments: "Sarah, remember what happened when you touched Mommy's 'straightener'?" And three-year-old Sarah instantly recalls the lesson learned from a burned finger. Other lessons can range from working through preadolescent peer group betrayal to that seventeen-year-old's learning the importance of oil to a car's engine.

We get to point out the larger picture of our children's lives. Our role as parents is to be the facilitator of those lessons, to identify the reason behind a "horrific, terribly no good, very bad day." Parents can help their kids work through the pain and grow in the process.

Some might consider the big-picture view as "salvaging" an experience, making the most of a tough day. On the other hand, if a vital lesson is absorbed, internalized, and the kid grows up a little more from the pain and processing with a parent, then it's been a great day after all.

Pain happens through every stage:

Preschool

- Skinned knees
- Death of a bug (or frog or fish)

School-age

- Lost a game
- Bike wreck
- Death of a pet

Preadolescence

- Betrayal of a friend
- Ridicule from peers
- Friends who move away
- Separation from friends by moving

Adolescence

- Death of a grandparent
- Failed test
- First breakup

College

- Didn't get accepted in college of choice
- Broken heart
- Death of a friend

Warning: Sometimes your child will hurt, and you just plain won't have an answer. A lot of the world's sorrow defies explanation, advice, and reason. If you can't explain the *why* of a painful situation, you can still explain the *who*. Show them the truth about God and His promise never to leave us. Teach them that God is still in control and He has a plan through the hurt. Allow them to grieve, but gently speak spiritual truth into their lives

Is it hard for parents to allow their kids to experience pain? LifeWay Research found that it is for some. Six out of ten parents want their children to experience pain and disappointment so they learn from it, while four out of ten try to protect them from this whenever they can.

Protecting Kids from Pain and Disappointment

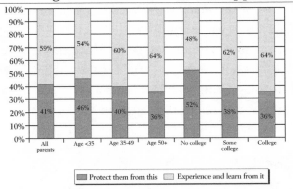

Figure 1. Protecting Kids from Pain and Disappointment

Calm in the Storm

Luke 8:22–25 is an example of Jesus taking a painfully frightening experience and creating an excellent teachable moment (as only the Master Teacher can!). Jesus was in the boat with His disciples when He decided to go to sleep. A huge storm came, and the boat appeared ready to sink. They were going down for the last time when one or more of the disciples screamed at Jesus out of their fear and pain. Jesus woke up, calmed the sea, and asked them where their faith had gone. The Lord's lesson? Threefold (at least):

> **Six out of ten parents want their children to experience pain and disappointment so they can learn from it, while four out of ten try to protect them from this whenever they can.**
>
> **–LifeWay Research**

1. Storms will happen in your life, but I will be with you through them.

2. I am stronger than any storm you will encounter.

3. Even when you don't see Me working right away (on your time schedule), trust Me in the storm.

Jesus seized an opportunity to teach a lesson they'd remember the rest of their lives! This lesson would not have been so memorable and meaningful to them had they not experienced the pain of the storm. But they did go through it, and, as a result, they kept the lesson of Jesus' power with them throughout their lives.

More Biblical Pain

God's Word gives us many examples of people who experienced pain.

Pain of Sin (Psalm 51). King David had an affair, killed his mistress's husband, and lost his child. Worst of all, he wounded his walk with God. David gave us an incredible example of repentance and restoration. His son Solomon also became the wisest king in the history of the world.

Possible Physical Pain (2 Corinthians 12:7–10). Paul had a thorn in the flesh. Though Paul begged the Lord to remove his pain, God did not. Paul praised and acknowledged God's power in his weakness.

Pain of Loss of Loved One (John 11:1–30). Lazarus, the brother of Mary and Martha, died. Jesus wept alongside the grieving sisters. He eventually displayed His power as Messiah and raised Lazarus from the grave.

Pain in Obedience to God (Matthew 26:36–39). Anticipating the agony of the cross in the garden of Gethsemane, Jesus understood clearly the pain He was about to endure. He asked God to let the cup pass but ultimately surrendered to His Father's will, bringing salvation to us.

Parent as Teacher

Communication, support, and perspective are important parts of teaching your children to manage pain. Beyond lessons and encouragement, however, your children learn how to handle stress, heartbreak, and disappointment by watching you. You model pain management through the storms in your life. No, you don't have to do it perfectly. Neither do you need to create needless anxiety by sharing every little detail. But honest and open communication about *your* crisis can speak volumes to them about how to manage tough times of their own.

From the LifeWay Research parenting survey, we learn that about three out of four parents said they try to keep their own pain away from their children. Forty-seven percent agree somewhat and 27 percent strongly agree with the statement: You try to keep your

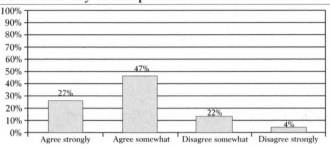

Figure 2. Do Parents Try to Keep Their Pain from Their Kids?

pain away from your child/children and not let them know what you are going through.

Tommy Lasorda, longtime manager of the Los Angeles Dodgers, was known to say that he "bled Dodger blue." As Tommy's loyalty showed when he bled, our true character is revealed when we show our pain.

Don't underestimate the impact your pain can have on your kids. I (Scott) recall a time when my dad went to tears as our family was together for prayer before bedtime. My dad taught in a community college in Minnesota for seventeen years and felt God was leading him to stop teaching accounting and start doing it for a missionary-sending agency in Philadelphia. As my mom struggled with this idea, my dad was overcome with the pain of wanting to follow God's will but also for our family to be together. These values of following God and valuing family created a memorable lesson I probably would not have caught without his showing his pain.

My son, Max, surprised us at the dinner table recently by saying, "Daddy, remember when you cried when you were praying?" At age six Max had suddenly recalled a moment from more than two years earlier.

Like my parents, Debbie and I pray with our kids each night before they go to bed. One night as I shared with them that my grandpa had died that day, I broke into tears for several minutes. Madison and Max simply asked why I was crying.

While this was not an easy time to talk, it was a valuable opportunity to communicate my love for my grandpa and that I would miss him. More importantly I was able to share that I was sure he was in heaven because he depended on Jesus Christ. That teachable time would not have occurred or made such an impression on my son if I had not shared my pain.

Here is another example of teaching through your pain: whether good or bad, your marriage can form lasting impressions on your children. Let's play out two scenarios:

Scenario 1. If your marriage is in a horrible state, one of your best parenting moments may be right around the corner. For example, for you two to seek help, turn your marriage around in the midst of its stormy state, could send a powerful positive message to your kids. Working through your problems can communicate to children God's healing power, not to mention your persistence in working through your difficulties. Years later, should they struggle in their own marriages, they can remember how you two stuck it out and worked through your problems. They can be encouraged by the lessons your marriage taught them.

Scenario 2. Same marriage. Same horrible state. But this time, the marriage doesn't survive. Teaching opportunities abound in this scenario, too. Partners can't control their mates and "make" them stay in a marriage. Let's say your mate walks out, leaving you and the family. You can still model for your kids what to do when the storms of life hit. Your children can see you taking God's promise of James 4:8 to heart: "Draw near to God, and He will draw near to you." They will see you leaning on Him, trusting Him through the storm. That kind of modeling can teach them for life as well.

When they watch you going through your pain in a healthy manner, they witness ways to stay faithful to God through the storm. Don't get confused: You never need to put on a fake smile and an "everything's fine" front. Your kids can see you hurt, deeply hurt, but still watch you honor your commitment to God and His Word in the middle of the pain. You also don't have to hurt alone. When your kids see you lean on your spouse, friends, counselors, and mentors during tough times, they learn to give and receive care and support from others. Later in their lives, when painful rain falls on them, your children will take courage from how you modeled spiritual wisdom and strength in life's storms.

Modeling Pain from Nana

We are in the middle of a painful time in our family right now. My (Rodney's) dad had a major stroke more than a year ago. Before he died, Dad was completely paralyzed, unable to speak or move for many months before he finally, at age eighty, went to be with the Lord.

My mom is in her eighties now and suffers from crippling arthritis. She spends most of her time in a wheelchair. She is weak, and most of her days are filled with pain. Mom and Dad were married for sixty-three years. In the middle of this rough spot, God was and is so real to us. He has answered so many prayers. Throughout his final months Dad was in a wonderful care facility with a loving staff—a miracle. God led us to a wonderful Christian lady to stay with my mom at night—a miracle.

There is so much pain, so much we don't understand, but we are learning every day to trust God. Yet one of the most memorable and beautiful things for us to see and our children to see is how Mom loved Dad. Dad couldn't give Mom anything—not a smile, not a word, not a touch. On rare occasions he would make eye contact for a few minutes.

Yet Mom got all dressed up to go see him and touch him with her crippled hands. She would sing and whisper to him of her love and prayers for him. She would tuck the sheets around him and fuss over him, making sure the nurses knew that he was her treasured husband.

Painful. Beautiful. I am so thankful that our adult daughters, one married herself now, saw modeled for them a marriage and love as only our God can give—unconditional, agape love.

Upon being fired from one head coaching position, NFL coach Tony Dungy said: "I think people look more closely at our actions in the rough times, when the emotions are raw and our guard is down. That's when our true character shows and we find out if our faith is real. If I'm going to call myself a Christian, I have to honor Jesus in the disappointments, too."[1]

The Pain of Regret

When our girls were little, we moved into a new home. There were four or five huge trees, all clumped together, just a few feet

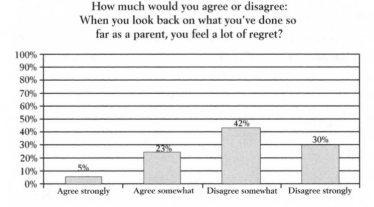

Do Parents Have Regrets?

How much would you agree or disagree:
When you look back on what you've done so
far as a parent, you feel a lot of regret?

Figure 3. Do Parents Have Regrets?

beyond our deck. I (Rodney) always intended to build my girls a tree house in the middle of those trees. It was a perfect setting to build it, and they kept asking for one. But time and life kept slipping away, and the tree house never happened. (My only hope of redemption is to build it for the grandkids, but, trust me, no promises!)

A broken promise to my girls? That hurt! It was painful for me. Notice I said "was" because after seven years of therapy I'm doing much better with it. (Just kidding.) Every parent has some kind of "tree house" story in their past. Like pain, the question is not whether parents will have regrets, but rather *when* regret comes, how do we manage it as parents? Our past mistakes can cripple us, rendering us helpless to attempt any kind of parenting effort at all. Confidence can bottom out every time we think of what we should or shouldn't have done in our parenting past.

When you find yourself about to drown in the vat of regret, here are two responses that can help.

1. Face the Regret

To fight regret, sometimes you have to be man or woman enough to look your kids right in the eye (maybe ask them to look at your nose!) and ask them to forgive you. You'll find power in a humble apology. Seeking forgiveness tells your kid that you know you are not perfect and mess up sometimes.

A parent can blow it at any stage. About two months after our first daughter was married, Jen and David visited our home late one night. Selma had already gone to bed. Jen was laughing with her sister, Natalie. Laughing, in my opinion, a little too loudly. I (Rodney) stated in a soft but fatherly stern (perhaps condescending) voice that if they didn't hush, they were going to wake their mom.

Immediately I saw the look in Jennifer's eye and knew I had crossed a line. I also knew I would never have spoken to any other wife like that in front of her husband. The third thing I knew was that I would have to apologize to her, as I did in front of her husband. (For a guy who had just blown it, I sure knew a lot!) And just as she had done for the last twenty-plus years, when I apologized to her, she quickly forgave me.

When necessary, no matter how long it has been, seek forgiveness from your kid. The tree house episode has long been forgiven. Yes, it is tough and risky. You will be vulnerable for sure. And yet you will be making a huge statement of honesty and love when you take that step.

Our pastor, Pat Hood, reminds us every week that he sins, and like Paul in Philippians 3:13, he says, "I do not consider myself to have taken hold of it" (I don't have it all together). Every time he mentions something like that, he builds credibility and connects with the people.

When parents ask for forgiveness, they build the same credibility. They connect with their kids and learn to deal with the pain of regret.

2. Beware the Enemy

We have an enemy who wants us to fail as parents. He does not want us to experience the adventure of life and parenting that God has planned for us. God's purpose in our lives is for Him to be glorified in our lives. Satan's purpose is to rob God of His glory! He tries to take us out by spotlighting our past faults. Peter put it this way: "Be sober! Be on the alert! Your adversary, the Devil, is prowling around like a roaring lion, looking for anyone he can devour" (1 Pet. 5:8).

What's his most effective weapon? Deception. Here is how Jesus described him: "When he [the Devil] tells a lie, he speaks from his own nature, because he is a liar and the father of liars" (John 8:44). He tries to make us believe what is not true. If our guard is not up and we are not walking closely with the Lord, who is the Truth, we can find ourselves buying the lies he throws at us.

Regret can keep us out of the adventure with God. Just as Jesus used Scripture when combating the deceiver, so can we. We can battle through our imperfections and our regrets with the truth of God's Word. Here are some examples of deceit the enemy can throw at us, and some scriptural truths to use in response:

Deceit. You can't do anything as a parent because of how you've treated your kids in the past!

Truth. "Therefore if anyone is in Christ, there is a new creation; old things have passed away, and look, new things have come" (2 Cor. 5:17).

Deceit. How do you think you can build a relationship with your kid? Don't you remember how you screamed at her just last week?

Truth. "If we confess our sins, He is faithful and righteous to forgive us our sins and to cleanse us from all unrighteousness" (1 John 1:9).

Deceit. Why are *you* of all people trying to teach your kids anything about God? You lied to your kids, remember?

Truth. "But one thing I do: forgetting what is behind and reaching forward to what is ahead, I pursue as my goal the prize promised by God's heavenly call in Christ Jesus" (Phil. 3:13–14).

Deceit. You *must* believe my view of you—that you will never be a good parent—because you've believed it too long, all of your life!

> **The way parents parent also can help move their children toward a personal relationship with Jesus Christ. It is much easier to grasp the grace of God when children live with parents who relate to them in grace. Conversely, it is difficult to imagine that almighty God can be grace-filled when children seldom have seen that quality at home.**
>
> —Richard Ross, *Parenting with a Kingdom Purpose*

Truth. "The One who is in you is greater than the one who is in the world" (1 John 4:4).

Before you can claim the truth of Scripture, you have to have a relationship with God. Knowing Christ gives you access to these promises, this truth. He is life. He is confidence. He is the key to raising your family. He is everything!

If you would like to receive the gift of eternal life with God and begin to be a parent who puts Jesus at the center of your family, pray a prayer similar to this:

> *Dear God, I know I'm a sinner. I believe Your Son Jesus died to save me from my sins. I ask Your forgiveness for those sins and accept Your offer of eternal life. Thank You for forgiving me of all my sins. From this day forward I choose to follow You and call You the Lord of my life. Amen.*

Share this decision with your spouse, a local church minister, your Sunday school teacher, or a small group leader. Connect with a nearby church that can help you grow in your faith. Incidentally, this brief focus on how to become a Christian isn't a digression. It has everything to do with how to be a strong parent.

Teaching Spiritual Truths as You Go

Let's review again our parent adventure passage, this time from *The Message*:

> "Love GOD, your God, with your whole heart: love him with all that's in you, love him with all you've got! Write these commandments that I've given you today on your hearts. Get them inside of you and then get them inside your children. Talk about them wherever you are, sitting at home or walking in the street; talk about them from the time you get up in the morning to when you fall into bed at night." (Deut. 6:5–7)

In the middle of life, in the middle of the pain of this life, we can teach our children these truths:

"No one will be able to stand against you as long as you live. I will be with you, just as I was with Moses. I will not leave you or forsake you." (Josh. 1:5)

"I have told you these things so that in Me you may have peace. You will have suffering in this world. Be courageous! I have conquered the world." (John 16:33)

The Prayer Focus

Father, You know how much I want to protect my children from the pain and heartbreak of this life. But I know I can't. Thank You for being with me through so much loss and pain. Just as You are with me, I know You will be with my children. I pray You will protect them from the evil one as You taught us to pray. Help me to teach them the truth of who You are through every situation in life including the hurt and disappointment they will face. Give me wisdom to point them to You. Let my children see You in me. Amen.

Parent Adventures

1. What can you tell your child about how God has worked in your life through a painful experience?
2. Is anyone in your family currently experiencing pain? What three things can you do to help them through this pain?
3. What can you share with your child from God's Word to help them understand how God helps us through pain? (See passages mentioned in this session.)

4. How did you come to faith in Christ? Pick a time to share this with your kids.

QUESTIONS FOR DISCUSSION

1. Describe a painful situation your child has encountered recently. List one positive outcome of that experience.
2. Have you ever experienced a time in your life when you didn't get the part, didn't make the team, or didn't get the promotion? What did you learn from this experience?
3. What painful experiences has your child gone through? How did you work through them?
4. What are some regrets you have in your life? How do these regrets affect your parenting?

Chapter 6

Celebrate!

I will celebrate before the LORD.

—2 SAMUEL 6:21

The last thing I expected was a party. I (Rodney) had had a long day and an even longer commute home. I was exhausted, and it was only Tuesday. I enjoyed coming home from the office, but fellow parents understand that when you walk through the front door, work is hardly finished. Most evenings consisted of making dinner, cleaning up after dinner, getting the girls to take a bath, drying their long hair, helping with homework, and then going through the bedtime routine. This particular night, however, was anything but typical. When I walked through the door, my mood was immediately transformed.

My girls, all three of them, decided this night would be special. Decorations filled our living room and kitchen. The nice tablecloth covered the table along with the good china.

Celebration filled the air. On a weeknight! It wasn't anyone's birthday. I hadn't gotten a raise or a promotion. They just wanted to celebrate an ordinary, everyday event—Daddy's coming home!

> When asked what she'd change about her life, an elderly woman said, "I'd use my good china much more often."

This atmosphere certainly changed everything that evening. My tiredness from the day quickly faded, and my spirit was lifted. I quickly caught the joy of celebration my girls had created.

The Party Drawer

To help our family think "celebration," Selma created a party drawer. We have in our home an antique buffet table with two huge drawers. The bottom drawer eventually became the storehouse for everything party related. Selma kept her eye open for sales and stocked the drawer with balloons, streamers, crayons, markers, scissors, paper plates, a variety of napkins, and such. (Did we tell you that parent adventures are often messy?) Anyone in the family might declare "it's time to celebrate," and off we'd go.

Celebrate . . . in the Middle of Life

When we look around our world, we may encounter difficulty finding reasons to celebrate. Crises like poverty, the economy, wars, and global warming—not to mention your own family's trials and struggles—stare us in the face every day. Taking time out to celebrate the little joys of life might seem trivial or even irresponsible when the world is filled with so many problems and so much pain.

Inside the home, something always needs attention. The oil needs changing in your car. Your Internet connection is down again! (Been there.) And that slow drain in the bathtub—aughh! Your third-grade son's teacher called a conference because she said he did what? Throw in the rumors floating around your work about layoffs, and you find yourself rapidly climbing the stress scale.

Clearly, the world is full of big crises and small problems that need and deserve our attention. As parents, we have the responsibility to discuss age-appropriate issues with our children because God deeply cares about the world. We need to care for the poor, the hungry, the lonely, the sick, and people who do not know Christ.

Celebration, however, does not mean sweeping those concerns under the rug. Instead, celebration suggests that some things are worth taking time—in the middle of life—to recognize and enjoy. Sometimes for a moment. Sometimes for a weekend. Sometimes longer.

Extravagant Celebration

The Gospel of Matthew records the story of a woman who chose to celebrate over Jesus. Much to the anger and confusion of the disciples, she broke an expensive jar of oil and washed His feet. Jesus responded to their frustrations by chiding, "You always have the poor with you, but you do not always have Me" (Matt. 26:11). Jesus wasn't dismissing the poor, but He was saying, "Yes, you will always have other concerns, but for this moment I want to celebrate this woman's gesture." Two thousand years later we are still celebrating her act of worship and humility. (When Jesus sets a celebration in motion, it sticks!)

Celebration says that as life happens—the good, the bad, and the ugly—we will frequently choose to focus on the good. The other side of life is not ignored. Life's stuff has to be addressed. Yet it will not drown out the reasons to celebrate. As a family you periodically need to get off the worry-go-round and have some fun together.

Actually, the hardships and challenges of life make celebration all the more necessary. Life happens to all of

> Life happens on the way to doing something else.

us. He "sends rain on the righteous and the unrighteous" (Matt. 5:45). Sometimes we need temporarily to drop the pressures of life in order to celebrate a child's making her bed for the first time or a teenager's getting his learner's permit. We get to teach our kids to see the good in the middle of the rain.

Celebration in the Bible

God's Word is full of celebration! In fact, God bookends the entire Bible with some form of celebration. In Genesis, the first week in history, God saw all that He had created and essentially said, "This is good stuff." It was a moment of daily celebration.

Likewise, His Word ends with a great celebration, a new heaven and a new earth—a new Jerusalem with jewels for walls, the river of life, and Jesus inviting us to drink from it (see Rev. 21–22). Not your average party!

> God saw all that He had made, and it was very good. —Genesis 1:31

Check out the following celebrations from Scripture. Notice how many parties happened in the midst of challenging times.

Jesus' First Miracle (John 2)

Jesus attended a wedding feast where the hosts ran out of wine. At His mother's request Jesus turned water into wine. Why? So the blind could see? So lame people could walk? No. He'd do that later. For His first miracle, Jesus turned water into wine *so the celebration could continue!* What does this miracle reveal about Jesus and His heart for celebration?

The Return of the Prodigal (Luke 15)

A Jewish father grieved because his youngest son had taken his inheritance and left home. Daily the father watched the road, hoping the son would return home. Then one day the father saw him coming. Talk about a party waiting to happen! The celebration centered on the son's return. No accomplishments. No job well done. No productivity. Just a celebration of life. The older brother didn't get it. To the reluctant brother the dad said, "We'll settle all other worries later. For now let's celebrate that your brother, who we feared was dead, is alive."

David Dancing before the Ark of the Lord (2 Samuel 6)

When the ark of the covenant, representing God's presence with the people, returned to Jerusalem, King David celebrated. The ark was finally home, and David was beside himself. It was time to get happy. David's wife, Michal, however, clearly disapproved of his undignified display. In spite of "Debbie Downer," David declared, "I will celebrate before the LORD" (2 Sam. 6:21). Michal didn't get the favor of the king, even though he was her husband.

Psalms of Celebration

The psalmist gives us several examples of praise and celebration to God:

- *Celebration of God's Justice*
  I'm thanking you, GOD, from a full heart,
  I'm writing the book on your wonders.
  I'm whistling, laughing, and jumping for joy;
  I'm singing your song, High God.
  (Ps. 9:1–2 *The Message*)

- *Praise to the Creator*
  Rejoice in the LORD, you righteous ones;
  praise from the upright is beautiful.
  Praise the LORD with the lyre;
  make music to Him with a ten-stringed harp.
  Sing a new song to Him;
  play skillfully on the strings with a joyful shout.
  (Ps. 33:1–3)

- *Praise for the Lord's Works*
  The LORD's works are great,
  studied by all who delight in them.
  All that He does is splendid and majestic;
  His righteousness endures forever.
  He has caused His wonderful works to be remembered.
  (Ps. 111:2–4)

- *Praise for God's Greatness*
  I exalt You, my God the King,
  and praise Your name forever and ever.
  I will praise You every day;
  I will honor Your name forever and ever.
  Yahweh is great and is highly praised;
  His greatness is unsearchable.
  One generation will declare Your works to the next
  and will proclaim Your mighty acts.
  I will speak of Your glorious splendor
  and Your wonderful works. (Ps. 145:1–5)

Ecclesiastes 3 says there is "a time to weep and a time to laugh; a time to mourn and a time to dance" (v. 4). Solomon emphasized the need for balance in our lives. Parents need to strike the proper balance with their families. Don't get swept away in the day-to-day routines of life. Instead, like Jesus, David, the father of the prodigal, the psalmists, and numerous others, carve out frequent times and places to celebrate with your family. We have much to celebrate because of God!

Celebrating Outside the Lines

Have we already mentioned that the parent adventure can be messy? Well, celebrations can also mean sometimes coloring outside the lines.

For starters:

Preschoolers

- Play dress up with old clothes.
- Put on an apron and help to cook dinner.
- Display artwork around the house.

School-age Children

- Decorate the house.
- Make a surprise dinner for Mom and Dad.
- Invite the neighborhood children over for a party.

Preadolescent Children

- Invite friends for a just-for-fun sleepover.
- Eat pizza on the living room floor.

Adolescent Children

- Host a makeup party.
- Celebrate getting a learner's permit, first date, touring colleges.

College-Age Kids

- Celebrate getting ready to leave home.

Financing the Fun

Warning! Teaching your children to celebrate may be hazardous to your image! I (Selma) remember the girls saving their money to buy me a surprise for no special reason. Dad took them shopping, but they got to pick the surprise for Mom on their own. (Thanks, honey.) They were so excited. They wrapped the gift themselves, and we had a special evening of celebration just for me.

After a simple meal of macaroni and cheese, they presented me the gift. The girls hovered anxiously with eyes sparkling, unable to contain their excitement. To my . . . er . . . surprise, they had gotten me a huge pair of bright yellow earrings. One was a question mark, and one was an exclamation point! Yikes! Of course, I immediately put them on and had to wear them the very next day!

Who would have ever thought that a pair of earrings would be a tool God would use for me to share Him with others! If someone asked, I could tell them about my girls, our family, and ultimately about our faith in God who gives us reason to celebrate.

Ever heard the expression, "It's the thought that counts"? In a family celebration the thought is *exactly* what counts. Money is no object. Rather, money *shouldn't* be the object. For instance, when the girls were small, we celebrated report cards. We reflected on the ups and downs, the good and the bad of another six weeks, and we celebrated. Often our "celebrations" were merely a form of giving our girls some major attention. Sometimes we'd just hang out in the living room, give a prayer of thanks, and express how proud we were of them. Other times we'd go to their favorite kid's restaurant and lose ourselves playing games and eating too much pizza.

Our personal twist: the report card celebration happened every six weeks *regardless of their grades.* In fact, the party was planned before they ever shared the results. We celebrated their hard work, their schools and teachers, and how God had blessed them with the ability and opportunity to learn.

Granted, some celebrations will cost more than others, but don't make the celebration about how much money was spent. Instead, make it about the recognition and the opportunity to teach

> **Children laugh three hundred times a day. Adults average fifteen times a day!**

them about God in the moment, the "party" not to miss!

The more creative you are, the less emphasis money will demand. *How* you celebrate can outweigh *how much you spend* celebrating. Here are some more ways your family can operate in celebration mode:

Celebrate . . .

- your child's coming to know Christ!
- the first day of school
- when children lose their last baby tooth
- a parent's new job, raise, or promotion
- baptism
- braces off (gum, popcorn, for a night—everything they were never supposed to eat)
- when someone does something helpful without being asked
- a new pet
- the first time they read Scripture on their own without any instruction/guidance from you
- overcoming a fear (child sleeps with no night light, teenager stays home alone)
- ability to learn
- the first time they share their faith with a friend
- nature

- rainy days
- a new friend
- their first chapter book
- first dress-up event
- getting a learner's permit
- first date
- acceptance to college
- moving into the dorm

Celebrate through Their Eyes

Kids get excited over the craziest things. What brings them joy might not connect with you at all, but that's OK. Whether it affects you personally, sometimes you just need to celebrate anyway.

When Natalie was six years old, I (Rodney) missed her first game of a softball double-header but arrived between games. She saw me and with unlimited jubilation exclaimed, all in one breath, "Oh, Daddy, this is so much fun. I've struck out five times. I love playing softball!" We'd work on Natalie's swing later on, but at that moment I hugged her and shared in her excitement.

> Kids: They dance before they learn there is anything that isn't music.
>
> —Poet William Stafford

Recently, Natalie, now grown up and completing a medical internship in another city, called to share another unique accomplishment: "Dad, today I got to work with the doctors in the GI lab. I saw seven colonoscopies this morning. It was awesome!" Once again, it didn't add up to me, but it was time to celebrate!

Celebrating Change

Think back to the "yes home" chapter. Remember we studied that parents' natural response toward their kids' strange ideas is usually *no*. In Christ, we can rewire that default setting to think about the unusual and occasionally say yes. It's the same with change. The natural response to change is, "Let's keep things the way they are." The known seems better than the unknown. As parents, we often cling to the past age, grieve its passing, and gloomily dread the coming stage. In contrast, when we have an attitude of celebration, we can welcome change.

Dealing with change is one of the most valuable lessons we can teach our children. Besides the Lord Himself (Jesus Christ, the same yesterday, today and forever—Heb. 13:8), change is the only constant this life offers.

Parents who celebrate life changes portray a future-focused outlook on life. "We're excited about your going into kindergarten." Or, "It's going to be awesome having a thirteen-year-old in our home!" (Really? Yes, really!) Such encouragement can help kids anticipate (not dread) what lies ahead for them.

On the other hand, guys and girls can feel guilty when we tell them, "You're not my baby anymore," or, "I wish you were still little so I could hold you like I used to," or, "Oh no, we're going to have a teenager in the house." It is like the parent blames the child for growing up.

During our young parent days, we often sought counsel and wisdom from our friends, the Byrums. Their kids were older than Jennifer and Natalie. At one point Selma asked Faye (the mom), "How do you handle your kids leaving one phase and growing into another?" Her response became our mantra: "It's not really that hard. We just look at each phase as better than the one before."

This parent celebrated the change in her children's lives. Right then we claimed a similar attitude for our parenting. We were so grateful for our friends and their timeless wisdom.

We have always told our girls that their current stage of life was the best stage yet. We were blessed partly because we determined in advance to make it that way. The girls are grown now, and we still celebrate where they are in their lives. It is still the best stage yet! And grandchildren have yet to arrive!

I (Rodney) remember telling the girls when they were nine or ten, "Do I miss that toddler running around that I could just pick up and carry anywhere? Sometimes, but I wouldn't trade the times we have together now and the level of conversation we have now for anything! It's the best time yet!"

Perhaps they thought we were spinning the situation some, but they also knew that when they went from nine to preadolescence and from adolescence to college, we'd embrace the change at every life passage and celebrate along the way. No guilt there.

Certain passages a child goes through are more critical than others. When they go through puberty, for example, complete with body changes, voice changes, and attitude changes, insecurities can skyrocket. Often they do not like what's happening to their bodies or the rest of their life. And yet, when a parent says, "I am glad you are at this age. I wouldn't want you to be at any other stage than where you are right now," that affirmation can be a drink of cold water in the desert of preadolescence. A simple encouraging word can literally recharge your preteen's self-esteem.

Of course, not all change is fun and games. Can change be painful? Absolutely! Telling high school classmates good-bye on graduation night is not usually a piece of cake. But parents get to help their children see that God works the change for good, whether or not we understand it at the time. Whether the change is a kid's learning to take his own bath or telling a first-grade teacher good-bye at the end of the year, parents can teach that God is a positive part of the change happening in their kids' lives.

The Pony Effect

I once heard a story about two totally different brothers. One boy was an extreme pessimist while the other was exactly the opposite. For the optimist, his parents put him in a room full of manure—only manure—just to see how his optimism would respond. (Do not try this at home!) After a while they checked on him. He was gleefully covered in manure and appeared to be playing in the stuff. They asked him why he was so happy. His response: "I haven't found him yet, but with all this manure, there's a pony in here somewhere!"

Sometimes parents need to embrace "the pony effect," the good in a challenging situation. Surprisingly, a recent president drew leadership principles from this story. In the midst of debating a tough issue, someone on his staff would often say, "Let's keep looking at this. There's a pony in here somewhere."

When your child turns two and learns the word *no*, remind yourself of the pony when you want to panic. When preadolescence creeps in, when puberty strikes, look for the pony. There's some good at every stage they enter and exit. God has promised good in all things for those who love Him. "We know that all things work together for the good of those who love God: those who are called according to His purpose" (Rom. 8:28). *All* means "all." Even when the change in your child's life is not pleasant, God works in it for His good. God's Word assures us that at whatever stage we find the parent-kid relationship, there's a pony in there somewhere. Find it. Point it out to your kid. Ask God to open your eyes to find the good in every difficult situation.

The Power of Celebration

As previously discussed, our family loved to empty our celebration drawer. Little did I know how God would use celebration to drive home a profound spiritual truth through our younger daughter, Natalie.

I (Selma) mentioned in a previous chapter that my mother died of cancer. For the last several months of her life, our family spent a great deal of time with Nana. On the last week of her life, Jennifer, nine, was away at a girls' camp while Natalie, seven, and I went to spend a week with Mom. Mom was confined to bed and her body was frail, but we had so many precious moments during that week.

As I prepared to leave her for what would be the last time, I kissed Mom good-bye. I can still see her smile and hear her whisper, "I love you." Early the next morning Rodney and I were still in bed when the call came. Mom had died peacefully in the early hours of the morning.

I was crying, and Natalie must have heard us because she came in our room and crawled up in bed with us. We held her and told her about her Nana. She slipped out of bed and went in the other room. I wasn't sure what she was doing, but soon she came back with a picture. She had been to the party drawer because she knew all about celebrations.

She handed me a picture she had drawn, and with the biggest smile I have ever seen, she said "Mommy, Nana is in heaven now running and playing, see!" The picture was of a big party complete with a welcome banner, balloons, and streamers. That picture stayed on the refrigerator for a long time (like all great works of art from children) and remains in our memories as a constant reminder of why we celebrate.

Teaching Spiritual Truth as You Go

The greatest celebration centers on God's love for us. He loved us so much that He sent His one and only Son to die for us (see John 3:16). We can have life, and we have it abundantly through Jesus (see John 10:10). We get eternal life because of Jesus! God created us, Jesus died for us, and God sent His Spirit to live in us. Celebration? You bet! Luke 15:10 says, "There is joy in the presence of God's angels over one sinner who repents." I'm pretty sure heaven knows how to throw a party. We have so much to celebrate! All that God is, all that He has done, and all that He has yet to do!

As you go, remind your child:

- *She was created in God's image!*
  So God created man in His own image;
  He created him in the image of God;
  He created them male and female. (Gen. 1:27)

- *God will give your son strength!*
  Do you not know?
  Have you not heard?
  Yahweh is the everlasting God,
  the Creator of the whole earth.
  He never grows faint or weary;
  there is no limit to His understanding.
  He gives strength to the weary
  and strengthens the powerless. (Isa. 40:28–29)

- *God loves your sons and daughters so much that He died for them!*
  For God loved the world in this way: He gave His One and Only Son, so that everyone who believes in Him will not perish but have eternal life. (John 3:16)

In the everyday stuff of life, you have daily opportunities with your children to celebrate. Let's go back and look again at the core verse for this study. (Maybe you will want to memorize this passage.) "Love the LORD your God with all your heart, with all your soul, and with all your strength. These words that I am giving you today are to be in your heart. Repeat them to your children. Talk about them when you sit in your house and when you walk along the road, when you lie down and when you get up" (Deut. 6:5–7).

The Prayer Focus

Father, I praise You. You are glorious and wonderful.
The works of Your hands amaze and astound me. I celebrate
even now the work of salvation You have brought to my life.
Father, help me teach my children to celebrate life because of You.
May they see in me the wonder of You. I pray my children
will know You and surrender to You. Amen.

Parent Adventures

1. What are three things you can celebrate with your children this week?
2. What can you tell your child about God's work in your life that causes you to celebrate?
3. Find a verse in God's Word to express your celebration of God. Look through this chapter for some ideas.

QUESTIONS FOR DISCUSSION

1. How does your family celebrate?
2. What causes your family to celebrate?
3. What is the biggest challenge facing families today?
4. What specific challenges does your family face right now?
5. Remember a special gift from your childhood that didn't cost a great deal of money but was special to you. What made it special?
6. What can you celebrate in your child's life right now?
7. Why is change often difficult to deal with?
8. Think about where your child is now. What is great about this stage of his/her life?
9. What are some changes you face right now?
10. What are some specific changes your children are experiencing?
11. How are you feeling about these changes?
12. Describe a time you experienced something good in the middle of a difficult time with your child.
13. What is a challenge in your parenting right now?
14. Do you see anything good that could come from this challenge?

Part II

The Church Challenge

Parents are responsible for the faith development of their children, but that is not a role we as parents have to do on our own. Churches have the privilege and opportunity to partner with parents in spiritual formation.

Part II of *The Parent Adventure* continues to look at information provided from a survey of American parents conducted by LifeWay Research. This in-depth research project provides substantial information about the state of parenting, according to the parents themselves, in the United States today. Both parents and church leaders will benefit from this snapshot of American parents as it reveals opportunities for us and our churches to encourage and equip other parents.

When churches equip parents, those parents are better prepared, in turn, to teach their children. Part II of *The Parent Adventure* looks at the link between home and church, the partnership between parents and church leaders in nurturing children to become believers, lifelong Christ followers.

Chapter 7

The Church's Role

*Teach a youth about the way he should go; even when he is
old he will not depart from it.*

—PROVERBS 22:6

onny Rockwell, a parent in Oklahoma, writes: "I don't need
you (the church) to babysit my kids or to entertain them.
For me, as a parent who understands my God-given role
and responsibility as a parent, I don't need you to focus so much
on coming up with some cool new way to minister to my children.
I need you to help me. Provide those cool new ways of doing ministry to me and my family. Minister to us as a family. Equip me to
teach, to lead, and to train my kids the way God would have me
do. Help me avoid being legalistic, yet lead me to help them see
and understand the reasoning behind decisions we are making as
parents. Help me to help them see everything through God's eyes.

Help me to provide a loving home environment where they catch a passion for God and surrender themselves to Him."

Donny gives voice to parents everywhere who want to partner with the church in raising their kids to be people of faith. That's what this part of the book is all about. We've looked at the parents' role. Now we'll look at the church's role and how parents and churches can work together.

If you are a parent reading the second half of this book, you may be asking:

- How can the church help me become a better parent?
- What are other American parents doing about teaching their children what they need to know in order to succeed in life?
- Do I have a responsibility to help other parents?

You may be a church leader (and perhaps also a parent) reading this book and asking:

- Do parents see themselves as responsible for their children's spiritual development, or do they think that's the church's job?
- How can we do a better job of partnering with parents to pass on their faith to the next generation, teaching them God's Word and how to live a missional life?
- What are other churches doing to help parents and families?

In the book *Made to Stick*, authors Chip Heath and Dan Heath examine "why some ideas survive and others die." They point out that not everything we think is true really is. They asked which of the following events kill more people in the United States: homicides or suicides, floods or tuberculosis, tornadoes or asthma, deer or sharks. The answers—suicide, tuberculosis, asthma, and deer—surprised many people. According to the authors, "People often trust their intuition, but our intuition is flawed by identifiable biases. Still, most people feel pretty good about their intuition, and it's hard to convince them otherwise."[1]

When asked, people tend to have opinions, based on intuition, about parenting—how they parent, where they get parenting advice, and the current state of parenting in the United States.

Rather than go with our intuition, we turned to LifeWay Research to learn about the state of parenting, what parents are saying about their own parenting adventures, in America today. You'll find answers to the questions that opened this chapter and more as we look at the research findings, the role God has given the church, and what some churches are doing in their ministry to parents.[2]

Parenting doesn't come with a how-to manual that explains exactly what to do in every situation of your child's life, but, as you realized from reading Part I, you began preparing for that role long before your first child was born. In fact, throughout your life you've been packing away elements that will impact what you do as you travel through the parenting adventure.

• Your own childhood experiences affect how you parent, both what you do and what you choose not to do.

• What you have observed in life is packed away to pull out as needed on this journey—the child screaming in the supermarket and the parent who angrily responds, the child and parent sitting together in church and sharing a hymnal even before the child can read, the family in the park taking time out for a picnic. All these stored images will impact your own plan for parenting.

• Who you are as a person, your preferences, your strengths and weaknesses, your fears and triumphs, and your life experiences will influence who you are as a parent.

• Who you are in your own faith walk and where you are in your own relationship with God will determine your desire to develop parenting skills based on biblical truths and your desire to guide your child's spiritual formation.

The parenting adventure begins to take shape long before it begins. But wherever you are on this journey—in the family planning stage or with teenagers in your home—you can make the adventure more positive for everyone by beginning or continuing to teach your children biblical truths, by applying the ideas you've learned in Part I of *The Parent Adventure* and by partnering with your church in this great adventure.

You've already benefited from biblically based ideas in this book that may even now be making a difference in your home. Further

> If you are a church leader, you can learn more about parenting needs and the current state of parenting in the United States, and you can explore ways to partner with parents to teach a child "about the way he should go" so that "even when he is old he will not depart from it" (Prov. 22:6).

understanding from research, reading what some churches are doing, and working with your own church leaders to adapt some ideas in your church can multiply the parenting benefits for you and other parents in your church and community.

The intent of Part II of this book is to provide some ideas for churches and parents working together, but the ultimate goal continues to be to draw parents to the Bible as the authority—the real how-to manual for parenting. God's Word keeps providing answers. His Word always offers something more every time parents return to its pages. Paul wrote to Timothy, "If I should be delayed, I have written so that you will know how people ought to act in God's household, which is the church of the living God, the pillar and foundation of the truth" (1 Tim. 3:15). That foundational truth is belief in Jesus Christ as Savior; Jesus said, "I am the way, the truth, and the life. No one comes to the Father except through Me" (John 14:6). Using God's Word as a guide, parents and churches can truly work together to raise children who also turn to God and to His Word as life's primary beacon, a lighthouse that provides safe direction throughout life.

I (Scott) have had poison ivy more times than I can remember. For years I tried ointments, home remedies, and even steroids prescribed by my doctor. These primarily treated my body's allergic reaction to the plant's oil. But the itch persisted and the rash spread, lasting a couple weeks at a time. I kept scratching and searching for a solution to the itch rather than trying to remove the oil that caused the reaction. Finally I found a soap that with some effort removes the oil that causes the allergic reaction.

Similarly, parents who are hurting will keep searching for a solution to deal with the symptoms of the problem that at least diminishes the persistent irritation. The Bible is not a quick-fix to stop an itch. It reveals the underlying problems and purpose of your family life. It is the authoritative source that leads to God. The One who

> **Parents are often so busy with the physical rearing of children that they miss the glory of parenthood just as the grandeur of the trees is lost when raking leaves.**
>
> —Marcelene Cox

created the family as the earth's first institution wants to work with parents and churches to raise children in the best possible way. This is what we read in Genesis, at the very beginning of the Bible:

This is why a man leaves his father and mother and bonds with his wife, and they become one flesh. (Gen. 2:24)

Adam named his wife Eve because she was the mother of all the living. (Gen. 3:20)

Adam knew his wife Eve intimately, and she conceived and gave birth to Cain. She said, "I have had a male child with the Lord's help." Then she also gave birth to his brother Abel. (Gen. 4:1–2)

The needs, the very real needs, of families today require more than a quick fix to solve the problems they face. They need the daily assurance that God ordained the family, and He still cares about your family today. You may turn to God's Word regularly as a guide for life and still not have thought of it as a resource for parenting. Yet it is filled with God's plan for your family and your life. This second half of *The Parent Adventure* will give you even more ideas for turning to God's Word and partnering with the church to address your own greatest needs as a parent.

Now let's begin to look at some of the research findings.

What Is the State of the American Family?

Half of all families in the United Sates do not remain intact. Children of those families are then raised in single-parent homes, in homes where one of the adults is not a biological parent, in a stepfamily, alternating between living with a mother and a father or living with other relatives.

Two out of three parents are currently married. Ten percent have never been married while the remaining 21 percent were previously married (not having remarried) or are separated.

Adults readily admit they have not done well at keeping their families intact: a total of 42 percent experienced separation or divorce, the death of a spouse, or getting married during the time they had children. Yet these significant changes were not isolated interruptions to family bliss. In fact, very few parents rate their families as "excellent" in key areas. When so much is changing in our lives and our culture, it is reassuring to know that we can live with the confidence that God and His Word never change. God's Word is true for all people, at all times. Those who call on God's name find peace, and only through a relationship with God can we embrace life fully.

Billy Crow, a pastor of a church in Clinton, Arkansas, says that his church has chosen to address the need for better marriages before focusing on parenting needs because stronger marriages are a foundation for better parenting. The church has provided four studies for marriage enrichment, targeting young couples, some with children, and some who do not yet have children. About half the couples have come from inside the church and the other half from other churches in the area and the community. As part of the studies, couples talk about what they are currently facing. They develop supportive relationships and encourage one another. From this foundation the church plans to move into offering parenting studies.[3]

Marriage also impacts a child's perception of church. We in LifeWay Research conducted a study of young adults who had attended a Protestant church regularly for at least a year in high school. One of the greatest predictors of the young person's continuing to attend church regularly between ages eighteen and twenty-two is that at age seventeen the child's parents are still

MARRIAGE

One of the greatest ways we can connect our kids to God is by having a strong marriage. Show your child God's love through your marriage. See lifeway.com/marriage for resources to help you build a strong marriage.

married to each other and both attend the same church. When our faith impacts our relationship with our spouse and we value the fellowship, worship, and service with other believers at church, these factors impact our children. Their own faith and perceptions of church are informed by what they see lived out at home. While stepfamilies are not reflected in this particular statistic, they have the same opportunity to model the impact of their faith on their marriage and church relationships.

All parents can model a healthy relationship with God as they go. Despite the ability to use factors such as marriage to predict a child's future behavior, these environmental indicators can be and are overcome. We found many young people who had "ideal" homes who stopped attending church, as well as many who seemed to have everything going against them who stayed in church. In the end, we have the responsibility to be faithful in our role as parents as we simultaneously trust God's power, plan, and purposes for our children's future.

Who Is Responsible for Encouraging a Child's Faith?

In spite of the divorce rate and adults' admission of failing in some ways, most say they are making a consistent effort to be better parents. Not only do most parents want to do a good job and seek to do a better job, but also they believe they are responsible for their children's spiritual development. They have not abdicated that specific responsibility to the church, school, or other relatives, or even left the children to find spiritual direction on their own. In fact, the vast majority of parents (83 percent) believe that parents are most responsible for a child's spiritual development.

This statistic may come as a surprise to some age-group ministers and leaders who think parents turn to the church for their child's spiritual formation. And, in fact, a lot of age-group ministers

The Child's Spiritual Development

In your opinion, who should be most responsible
for a child's spiritual development?

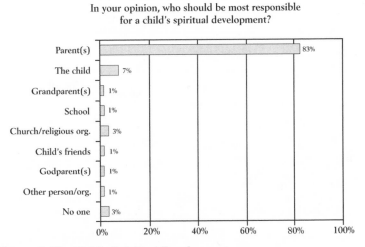

Figure 1. The Child's Spiritual Development

through the years have accepted that responsibility. This survey clearly shows that parents see their children's development as the parents' responsibility.

While parents agree that their children's spiritual formation is their responsibility, most parents don't rate their family as having a healthy spiritual life. In fact, of all the areas evaluated, spiritual life was one of the lowest rated areas. Only 13 percent said their family's spiritual life is excellent, while 57 percent called it good or very good.

In completing her doctoral work, Jeanne Burns, a preschool minister in Springfield, Missouri, worked on a project about faith development. Her findings were consistent with the results of LifeWay Research's parenting survey. Consistently parents agreed that they were responsible for their children's spiritual formation and development. The problem, however, is that parents are so busy that they are not taking the time to find out how to help their children grow spiritually. Jeanne's own daughter admits that she often turns to the Internet for help.

Many Scriptures echo the admonishment to parents in Proverbs 22:6 to "teach a youth about the way he should go," but the Bible also reveals a role for the church in developing all believers regardless of their age. In Ephesians, the apostle Paul described how the body of Christ, the church, is to function.

> And He personally gave some to be apostles, some prophets, some evangelists, some pastors and teachers, for the training of the saints in the work of ministry, to build up the body of Christ, until we all reach unity in the faith and in the knowledge of God's Son, growing into a mature man with a stature measured by Christ's fullness. (Eph. 4:11–13)

Parents alone cannot begin to provide everything that is available through those Jesus Christ has gifted within a church. God brings these people together for the purpose of training the saints, including our children. Members' investment and involvement in ministry allow our children, teenagers, and young adults to become united in the faith and united with others in the church. God's plan is for the church to play an indispensable role in helping young believers grow into Christ's likeness. They are also a part of the body of believers who, as they grow and mature in unity, are measured by the fullness of Christ.

One middle-aged friend recently shared with us her memories of faith formation when she was a child. She recalls sitting on the floor while her mother ironed and talking about the Bible, God, Jesus, salvation, and doing what God wants us to do—every day and in a lifetime. At that time most clothes had to be ironed, and with a family of five (mom, dad, and three kids), there was always plenty of ironing to do and plenty of time for conversations about faith. Now her mother is in her eighties, and mother and daughter are still talking about faith formation and faithfulness. Her mom still never misses an opportunity to talk with children, grandchildren, great-grandchildren, and total strangers about how much she loves the Lord. Her children "rise up and call her blessed" (Prov. 31:28).

But what are parents today going to do? No one irons anymore. Parents are busy. Many want help, but help has to be on the run.

To help meet the help-in-a-moment demand, preschool minster Jeanne provides a variety of resources for busy parents:

• Once-a-month Wednesday sessions address popular topics such as love languages; personality types; learning styles; age-appropriate physical, mental, social, and spiritual development; and how parents can impact their kids through a better marriage relationship.

• Parenting books are located in the children's library. While children are browsing through books, parents can select a book or search for answers to a current question.

• Parents receive a quarterly newsletter from the church that includes new library resources, encouragement, parenting tips, a calendar of events, and a Q&A section. The tips often provide simple ideas for parents to include faith formation conversations or activities that fit with normal parent-child together times, taking advantage of teachable moments.

• The church includes more activities for children and parents together than "drop and run" activities for children that separate them from their parents. With parents and children together, leaders can involve parents in the faith development, teaching children and parents at the same time. Observing how parents and children interact with each other also gives age-group ministers and lay leaders greater understanding of each child.[4]

Clara Mae Van Brink, a psychiatric nurse and preschool leader, offers these tips for parenting events:

• Plan events when children are busy at church already. This has several benefits. The parents have to bring their children to the church anyway so they are likely to stay when something helpful is planned for them, and child care is already provided. Parents are too busy to commit the time for another church event. Leaders show their commitment to families by not planning events at times that keep parents away from their kids.

• Keep events short. If you plan a series of studies during Sunday school or on Sunday or Wednesday night, limit it to four to six weeks.

• Provide a viewing guide or a listening sheet for seminars. Parents won't take notes, and they won't read handouts. Giving them a listening sheet tells them that you expect them to take notes.

• Be prepared to help parents who want more. Develop a resource list of books you recommend and trust. Don't recommend a book you have not read. Or, enlist other parents to read and review books. That takes the edge off "needing" a book's advice, and parents will trust the recommendation of another parent. It also takes the pressure off the one leading an event to be an expert.

• Some people won't come to seminars or special events no matter what you do. If possible have backup audio or videotapes (CDs and DVDs) for parents who missed a session or for those who won't attend but will take time to look or listen at their own convenience.

• Keep seminars short. Two hours is about the maximum time parents will attend. Fitting seminars in during church class times is even better. If you are planning special events, consider offering them twice, once on Friday night and again on Saturday morning. Your attendance is likely to go up considerably. Parents and families like choices and appreciate your giving them options.

• Consider working with adult age-group leaders and teachers to provide a special parenting class once a quarter during the Sunday school time.

• Don't be discouraged if you start small. If a few couples buy in, the ministry to parents will grow.

• If you are an age-group minister, view yourself as a community minister. Offer classes at a YMCA. Offer classes through local schools' PTOs. Principals are usually happy to offer these. These classes are not hooked to a denomination, so the event can become an outreach ministry of your church. Always provide free childcare at this type of event.

• One way to get church and community parents to attend a parenting seminar is to tie it to a free fun event you are offering their children. Providing a free fun event for their children may be a greater hook than any education you can offer a parent.

• Don't try to be the expert. Enlist other people such as doctors, dieticians, teachers, and mental health experts. But be sure the experts you enlist are Christians. If you enlist experts to lead a seminar, continue to take part in the event as the age-group minister so that through the event you continue to build relationships with parents who attend.

• Parents often don't know a lot about basic growth and development, but they won't admit their lack of knowledge or a need to learn it. Avoid seminars built around basic themes. Offer instead seminars about birth order, for example. This is always a popular topic, and you can build in basic development content.

• Plan events that have applications in homes, businesses, or personal life such as time management or understanding personalities. Such topics are more likely to entice dads to attend.

• Focus on broad-stroke issues, and make every event fun.[5]

The more religious the parent, the more likely he or she is to say that parents should be most responsible for the child's spiritual

> Parents ready to assume this amazing responsibility need all the help and support they can get. Though church ministers and leaders are not the primary spiritual leaders of children, they can be powerful partners with parents ready to take on this role.
>
> —Richard Ross, *Parenting with Kingdom Purpose*

development. Among Evangelicals, 96 percent said that parents are most responsible for their child's spiritual development. Among the completely nonreligious, 21 percent said the child himself or herself should be most responsible.

Church leaders can celebrate the fact that so many parents today believe that a child's spiritual development is their responsibility. And while church leaders can wholeheartedly agree with parents that children should be guided in their spiritual development by their parents, this doesn't mean that the church doesn't play a significant role here. Parents bring their children to church or see that their children get to church as one way of being responsible for training their children spiritually. Parents often select a church based on how well that church will nurture their children, even sacrificing their own needs if they believe a particular church is the best place for their children.

Parents' acceptance of the responsibility for the spiritual development of their children should motivate church leaders to take

> We're too busy to spend time with God. Consequently, we don't know who God is, which means we don't know who we are. We then try to establish our values ourselves through fame or fortune, which causes us to be too busy.
>
> —Parent from Georgia

seriously their responsibility to teach children well the truths of the Bible and how to find salvation and live out their faith. It is also a warning to church leaders that a third of nonreligious parents don't feel at all responsible for directing the faith of their children. The church, while not having the authority or responsibility of the parents, can seek to fill the gap in spiritual development for children whose parents do not feel compelled to make spiritual formation a part of their responsibility as parents.

What Are Reliable Sources of Help for Parents?

This summer the McConnell family took a trip out West that included a morning at the Museum of the Rockies in Bozeman, Montana. Max raced from room to room to see what fossil or picture was around the corner while I tried to get at least a cursory look at the volume of information. The size of some items was staggering: a sauropod's leg bone was taller than Madison! The variety and the number of fossils they had on display that were primarily found in Montana and Wyoming were amazing. Yet with all of this information, the list of things expert paleontologists (people who study fossils) still do *not* know is much longer than the list of things they do know about the characteristics, habitat, and life of these dinosaurs. Some of the displays listed as many questions as facts. Clearly what is "known" today often requires evidence to be pieced together with theory or speculation that may change over time.

That's how a lot of parents approach information on parenting. They may find an idea or two to consider, or they may seek the answer to a specific need right now. But next week or next month or next year they will receive advice or read another book with an idea or two that may even contradict the last parenting book they read. They may have given up finding definitive answers and are content to function with the little they already know.

Role of Religious Faith in Parenting. Only a slim majority of parents indicate that their religious faith plays an important role in their parenting. Among the six possible answers, the responses are fairly evenly distributed with only 12 percent of all parents saying that their religious faith is the top influence in how they raise their children. Another 23 percent call it one of the most important influences. Almost a third of all parents either have no religious faith or say it has little or no influence on their parenting.

Sacred Texts as a Source of Advice. Only 14 percent of parents indicate that they are very familiar with what the Bible has to say about parenting. When asked where they get their parenting advice, by far the most common place for getting parenting advice was one's own experiences growing up, followed by parents, friends, and spouse. Only 21 percent said they get a lot of advice from a sacred text (the Bible, Koran, etc.).

Families face significant change. Survey results show that 42 percent of families have experienced significant structural change in their families. That alone suggests great need. Such changes can pile on pain, and often such changes mean a U-Haul is needed to carry the accumulated baggage from past experiences. The last thing these parents need is another theory or new anti-itch medicine. These families, all families, need a constant in their sea of change.

God's eternal Word is sure and endures from generation to generation. Parents can learn from what the apostle Paul wrote to young Timothy, his son in the faith. First, he celebrated the generation before Timothy who had nurtured him in his faith:

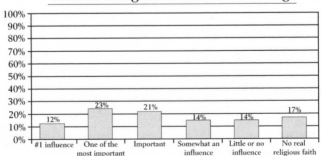

Figure 2. Role of Religious Faith in Parenting

"I thank God, whom I serve with a clear conscience as my forefathers did, when I constantly remember you in my prayers night and day. Remembering your tears, I long to see you so that I may be filled with joy, clearly recalling your sincere faith that first lived in your grandmother Lois, then in your mother Eunice, and that I am convinced is in you also" (2 Tim. 1:3–5). Later in this letter Paul wrote, "But as for you, continue in what you have learned and have become convinced of, because you know those from whom you learned it, and how from infancy you have known the holy Scriptures, which are able to make you wise for salvation through faith in Christ Jesus. All Scripture is God-breathed and is useful for teaching, rebuking, correcting and training in righteousness, so that the man of God may be thoroughly equipped for every good work" (2 Tim. 3:14–17 NIV).

In spite of the fact that most parents feel responsible for their children's spiritual formation, parents are turning to a failed standard to help with their parenting when they need to turn to the Bible. Many parents today grew up in dysfunctional homes, broken homes, yet they return to the only models they know for parenting—the homes in which they grew up. Even if they were dissatisfied with many of the ways their parents treated them as children, they use those same patterns in raising their children today. We looked at the way faith is handed down from generation to generation in the Bible, but more than faith is passed from one generation to the next. Dysfunctional patterns can just as easily be passed forward as can biblical truths. Parenting methodologies from the past are often cycles that should be broken rather than continued. And even in the healthiest homes, the Bible should be the authority, not what the last generation of parents did.

Parenting Advice and Encouragement. When asked about their need for help, guidance, or advice in parenting, three out of ten parents said they do not need any help or advice. Six out of ten said that help would be nice but they didn't really feel a huge need for help. About one out of ten said they really needed help in parenting. The less religious parents were, the less likely they were to say they need any help, guidance, or advice.

In terms of motivational help, only 15 percent said they really need more encouragement as a parent; 59 percent said encouragement would be nice but didn't perceive it as a big need. And 27 percent said that they already receive plenty of encouragement as parents. The same independence and reliance on personal experience is also seen in parents' attitudes toward encouragement.

Just 11 percent said they have nowhere to turn for encouragement. The most common sources of encouragement for parents were family—spouse or partner, parents, kids, or other family members. Among weekly churchgoers 38 percent did not get encouragement from a sacred text such as the Bible, and 24 percent said they got no parenting encouragement from their church. Over a third of born-again Christians got no encouragement from these religious sources.

Clearly the church has much to do in this area. Some churches are doing an excellent job of teaching the Bible to children and teenagers but little to help or encourage parents. In writing this book, we informally asked people how their churches were helping or encouraging them as parents, and often the response was, "It isn't." Sometimes regular churchgoers seemed a little surprised at their own answer, apparently feeling supported by the church in other areas of their life.

Who Lets Faith Influence Their Parenting?

When American parents were asked about their familiarity with what the Bible says about parenting, only 14 percent felt very familiar with what the Bible says about parenting. Among parents with evangelical beliefs, the number is better but still only 52 percent.

The challenge for parents and the church is clear. Parents can learn more about what the Bible has to say about parenting and how they can teach biblical truths to their children. And the church can do a much better job of helping parents, encouraging parents, and proving that the church is a valid source for helping parents. This is a potential win-win strategy for parents and churches. Parents want to improve their parenting skills, and the church can equip parents to take advantage of teachable moments with their children when they are motivated to learn.

> Only 14 percent of parents surveyed feel very familiar with what the Bible says about parenting.
>
> —LifeWay Research

The book *Essential Church* by Thom S. Rainer and Sam S. Rainer III has a lot to say about how generations pass on their faith. This research-based book focuses on young adults, and what this father-and-son writing team learned is that parents and the church currently aren't doing such a good job of passing on their faith. Even when parents took their children to church, often when those children become young adults they no longer attend church. Why? Because the church is not essential to their lives. One young man said, "Nothing big or negative caused me to stop attending church. . . . I just came to a point that I did not see church as essential to my life. And I guess that has been the case for over fifteen years now."[6] Clearly not only young adults are failing to see the church as essential. Even regular churchgoers do not always see the church as essential in helping them with their parenting skills. In teaching adults the Bible, church leaders and teachers can do a better job of applying biblical truths to the role of parenting.

Biblical Truth

Abraham, Isaac, and Jacob; Joshua; Eunice and Lois are all biblical examples for passing on their faith. But the Bible has some examples that aren't so commendable too. Samuel's job as a young child was to tell Eli that he had not adequately passed on his faith to his children.

> Eli's sons were wicked men; they had no regard for the LORD. . . .
>
> Now Eli was very old. He heard about everything his sons were doing to all Israel and how they were sleeping with the women who served at the entrance to the tent of meeting. He said to them, "Why are you doing these things? I have heard about your evil actions from all these people. No, my sons, the report I hear from the LORD's people is not good." . . . But they would not listen to their father. . . . By contrast, the boy Samuel grew in stature and in favor with the LORD and with men. (1 Sam. 2:12, 22–24, 26)
>
> The LORD said to Samuel, "I am about to do something in Israel that everyone who hears about it will shudder. On that day I will carry out against Eli everything I said about his family, from beginning to end. I told him that I am going to judge his family forever because of the iniquity he knows about: his sons are defiling the sanctuary, and he has not stopped them. Therefore, I have sworn to Eli's family: The iniquity of Eli's family will never be wiped out by either sacrifice or offering." (1 Sam. 3:11–14)

God takes seriously the parents' responsibility to pass on their faith to their children. He expects adults to walk in the way He directs and to keep passing on the faith.

"Love the LORD your God with all your heart, with all your soul, and with all your strength. These words that I am giving you today are to be in your heart. Repeat them to your children. Talk about them when you sit in your house and when you walk along the road, when you lie down and when you get up" (Deut. 6:5–7). These verses offer a challenge to parents and to the church. These words will continue to navigate us through *The Parent Adventure.* The greatest thing you can give your child is a love for God and an understanding that all of life is about Him. How assuring it is, however, to know that we do not have to do this in our own strength.

Paul echoed this instruction in 1 Thessalonians 4: "We ask and encourage you in the Lord Jesus, that as you have received from us how you must walk and please God—as you are doing—do so even more. For you know what commands we gave you through the Lord Jesus" (vv. 1–2). If you are a follower of Christ, you are to walk in the ways you have been taught and to teach those ways to others.

God's Spirit lives in you. God will teach you how to teach your children. The church, the body of Christ on earth, will also partner with you to help you as you seek to be a better parent, will teach you God's Word so that you can pass on biblical truths to your children, and will support you when you need a friend along the way in this parenting adventure.

The Prayer Focus

God, our Father, You created the family at the beginning of Your world. No one knows more about parenting than You. Thank You for the families in my church. Show us how to support one another on this parenting adventure. Give us light for our paths to raise our children in the way You would have them go. In Jesus' name, amen.

Parent Adventures

1. Think of a parent with a child the same age as your child. Select one or more topics about being a parent to a child of that age. Then invite your friend to coffee for a conversation. Can this conversation lead to occasional times of sharing?

2. If your friend is not a Christian, can it lead to sharing the gospel? If your friend is already a Christian, talk about where you get advice for parenting.

3. Share biblical truths that are important to each of you in parenting. Consider becoming parenting prayer partners for three months.

4. Partner with your friend in reading this book. You may want to read a chapter a week for three months. Share parent adventures and biblically based parenting ideas over coffee, a quick phone conversation, or even in an e-mail.

QUESTIONS FOR DISCUSSION

1. You may get parenting ideas from relatives or from your own childhood experiences. What were you taught as a child that has a biblical basis? What advice from your family do you get that has a biblical basis? You may have thought of some of the things you are teaching your children as family values when they are actually biblical truths. Family values are good. Biblical truths are certain and eternal. Hint: Look at the Ten Commandments (see Exod. 20), the Great Commandment (see Mark 12:29–30), and the Sermon on the Mount (see Matt. 5–7) for some of these teachable truths.

2. The Bible talks about giving us light for our path (see Ps. 119:105). That's light to see just what's in front of us, not to see to the end of the road. Jesus taught the disciples to pray about today (see Matt. 6:9–13). This chapter talks about your parenting "itch," your immediate need. Where do you need light for your path right now? What is your parenting need today? Who might have similar needs or perhaps be a little farther along in the parenting adventure to share light on where you are right now?

Chapter 8

Planning Together

For I know the plans I have for you.

—JEREMIAH 29:11

T he Boyd family—mom, dad, and two daughters—went on an international family missions trip, FamilyFEST. About the trip, Denise, the mom, writes: "My whole family—my husband, our two daughters, and I—went to FamilyFEST. I really wanted to go because my youngest daughter, Jamie, went two years ago, and I saw how it changed her life. After that, I really pushed for our whole family to go.

"We went to Juarez, Mexico, in June 2007. I'm a nurse, so while in Mexico I worked in one of the medical clinics. My husband helped replace a roof. My daughters worked in two different Vacation Bible Schools.

"One thing happened while we were there that really touched me as a mother. My oldest daughter is a real camera buff. She brought two cameras and planned to take as many pictures as possible. On the first day at one of the churches she took almost a full memory card of pictures. She put her camera on a backpack next to one of the other workers and went to play with the children. When she came back, her camera was gone. She was heartbroken, not so much about the camera but about the pictures. Later in the week she was in the home of one of the church families and saw the camera on the shelf. Several people were in the room, and she did not want to cause trouble. She spoke with one of the adults in the group, and they went together and spoke to the pastor. It turned out that it would have been a very touchy thing to get the camera back.

"The next day my daughter went to the pastor and took him the charger for the camera and told him they could keep the camera and maybe they could get some use out of it. I cry even now when I think of her willingness not only to give up her treasure but also to ensure that the church could use the camera. I learned so much about the kind of woman she is becoming. It meant the world to me. I also learned something about priorities myself. I would say our trip is one of the most meaningful things we have ever done as a family. I think it opened our eyes to the needs of others and how much we have. I think I can say the same for our whole family. We also met some lovely people. My daughter, Laura, will be home from college for her Christmas break in a couple of weeks. She is going to visit the family she met on our trip two days after she gets home. Our youngest daughter, Jamie, wants to go to Tijuana again next summer. I have to say going on FamilyFEST was one of the best decisions we ever made."[1]

The Boyds planned for this trip. It was important for them as a family to take a mission trip together. A parenting plan doesn't mean that before a baby is born the parents map out their family's journey for the next eighteen years. It does mean being intentional about some plans, like going to FamilyFEST. A parent plan is like a budget. It lays out goals and intentions but has flexibility to make changes along the way. With planning, parents are more likely to see their kids maturing, as Denise Boyd did. That means letting go, step by step, becomes a lot easier.

"Letting go" became a plan for our lives. With God's help and direction, we look at transitions as growing opportunities for our children and for us as well. And we are grateful that churches are planning ways to partner with parents. With a focus on a child's significant stages and transitions, parents can look at where their children have been and where they are going. They can prepare for the future, for letting go. With a "letting go" outlook, we can see how God is shaping our children and preparing them for His plan for their lives. And we can be grateful and excited to be a part of that plan.

But not all parents have a plan for "letting go" or, for that matter, anything else about parenting. In fact, nine out of ten parents do not have a written plan for parenting, and a third have no plan at all.

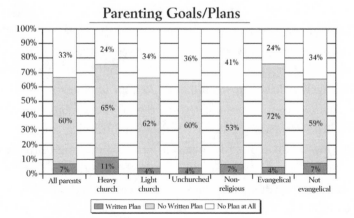

Figure 1. Parenting Goals/Plans

Our plan, at least part of our plan, was letting go. In order to have a plan, you have to have some sense of direction, some sense of where you want to end up on this parenting adventure. You can't plan without having a place to go. Of course, the start and end of that plan has to be Jesus Christ, "the Alpha and the Omega, the Beginning and the End" (Rev. 21:6).

> Just 7 percent of all parents have a written plan or goal for what they want to accomplish as a parent. Six out of ten have nothing written, but they do have clear goals in their minds. Parents who have a plan generally have a more positive parenting experience.
>
> —LifeWay Research

Developing a plan for "letting go" made a difference in our (Rodney and Selma) approach to raising our two girls, as well as other plans we made along the way. But does having a parenting plan really make a difference in the parenting adventure? According to LifeWay Research, the answer is yes. Parents who have a plan have more positive parenting experiences. They are more likely to refer to their parenting experiences as fun, energizing, and fulfilling. They are also more likely to have better communication, spend more time together as a family, treat one another with respect, focus more on family members' spiritual lives, and to say they feel fulfilled as parents.

However, parenting is about far more than feeling fulfilled. It is preparing our children to walk with God as they step out on their own. It is also helping our children connect to church in a way that they want to attend when it becomes their choice.

WHO HAS A PARENTING PLAN?
(AND WHO DOESN'T?)

- Younger parents are more likely to have a plan.
- The older the parent, the less likely he or she is to have a parenting plan.
- Nonwhite parents are more likely to have a parenting plan than whites.
- Parents who regularly attend worship services are more likely to have a parenting plan than those who attend infrequently.
- Parents who are born again are more likely to have a parenting plan than those who are not.
- Parents who have only male or only female children—including parents of only one child—are less likely to have a parenting plan than are parents with children of both genders.

How Churches Are Responding

Several "letting go" milestones occur at church and provide both the parent and others in the church with opportunities to help the child embrace the church as well as helping parents let go. These include:

- The first Sunday morning in the church nursery
- The first Sunday in congregational worship instead of preschool or children's worship
- The first overnight church camp or retreat
- The first youth group activity
- The first lock-in at church
- The first mission trip
- The first Sunday in a young adult small group instead of a youth class

While each of these milestones can mark a young person's development, they also are moments of decision. Children can have a bad experience or choose to have a bad attitude that easily can inhibit their development within the life of the church.

Here are suggestions from churches who are aware of the need to help parents let go and to help children embrace church:

Preschool

• Making a great first impression when a child is dropped off at preschool Sunday school is important to all concerned, and keeping the weekly greeting warm and inviting for the child reassures both child and parents.

• Plan a parent education class prior to baby and parent dedications. Even if parents have had more than one child, continue to include them in this life-event class. They may be more receptive to learn after the first child because of the challenges they have faced. And times change. During the dedication seminar church leaders can share with parents what their children will do during worship care and Sunday school. Leaders can tell about the steps they take to make sure their children are safe and loved. They can tell parents what their children can learn about God and the ways they begin to teach them at a very early age (Clara Mae Van Brink, a psychiatric nurse and preschool leader).

• When children are moving from preschool to elementary school, your church can present them with their first Bibles and plan an event for parents to let them know what is expected of their child and of the parents during this presentation in the church's worship service. At the same time explain that the Bible the children will receive is the same translation they will hear in Sunday school so if parents use that Bible with their children, children will hear the same words at home and at Sunday school. Tell parents about children's activities in Sunday school and kids' worship or about transitioning to the church's corporate worship and tips for parents in making that transition. Remind parents about children's physical and mental development and talk with them about how they can discern when children are ready to talk about making the decision to follow Jesus as Lord and Savior (Clara Mae Van Brink, a psychiatric nurse and preschool leader).

Children

• Plan intergenerational worship, education, ministry, and missions opportunities (not just recreation) events for parents and children. Parents can see how children are growing and learning. Parents can experience their children and teenagers as brothers and sisters in Christ in addition to their parent-child relationship.

• Plan opportunities for children to be away from parents such as day camps, summer camps, and weekend retreats so that children grow in independence from parents in a Christian environment and in positive church experiences.

Youth

• Help teenagers begin to discover their gifts by trying on different roles in church activities. Reward the experience without focusing on excellence. Let them discover on their own what kinds of roles they enjoy.

• Guide teenagers in finding ways to use their passions, interests, skills, and talents in and through the church. Help them to see that they are uniquely created in God's image and that He has a plan for each and every life.

• Include teenagers in leadership roles as soon as possible. Teenagers may serve as ushers, as student representatives on church planning teams, and in other roles.

Parents who see their children and teenagers growing in a variety of ways in the context of the church will feel better about letting their children go, stage by stage.

Parents are sometimes reluctant to ask for help. Many tend to see even attending a seminar as admitting that they are having problems. This goes back to the information we considered in chapter 7.

Parents tend to ask advice from family members or to relate to their children the way their parents related to them. Connecting seminars with life events helps take the edge off the "we need help" stigma.

Jay Strother, minister to emerging generations at Brentwood Baptist Church near Nashville, says that if you ask parents about the future of their kids, you get two responses: (1) Most parents respond that they want their kids to get into a really good college. (2) Many, especially those who are unchurched, are fearful about the future for their kids. Both of these responses are opportunities for the church.

Churches might partner with parents to help parents and kids with transitions and/or fears regarding:

- Going to college
- Getting a driver's license
- Going back to school in the fall

Transitions and fears of parents and kids are important to church leaders too. They can work together to deal with those fears. For example, here are some ideas churches can offer to deal with parents' concerns about their kids going to college:

1. Offer a small-group study during the spring or summer between high school and college with practical ideas—how to do laundry, how to balance a checkbook, the dangers of having a credit card, how to find a new church—as well as moral and spiritual truths—dealing with temptations in college, finding a Christian peer group, and so forth.

2. Establish prayer partners between senior adults and college-age students. Senior adult prayer partners may also send encouraging notes and e-mails, bake and send cookies, and regularly ask students for prayer concerns.

3. Churches can include students in worship when they are at home for school breaks. They can enlist them as youth leaders for

summer events. And they can continue to help them discover and use their gifts when they are in their home church.

A new generation of age-group ministers is rethinking their philosophy of ministry. Jay Strother says that when their church took a hard look at age-group ministries, they saw a lot of good ministries but not always the results they wanted. They decided that they wanted age-group ministries to work together toward the same goals. They asked themselves, "What is our long-term goal, and how are we going to get there?"

They were influenced in their thinking and planning by the four words that Thom Rainer and Eric Geiger used in *Simple Church*: *clarity, movement, alignment,* and *focus*.[2] They didn't want to keep adding ministries to meet the needs or fill the gaps they thought might be missing in age-group ministries. They began with a look at philosophy and structure and to rethink their entire age-group education and discipleship ministry. They reorganized the staff structure, asking Jay to move from his role as youth minister

> Imagine a church where you, as a leader, can articulate clearly how someone moves from being a new Christian to become a mature follower of Christ. Imagine that your church is no longer just busy but is alive with ministries and activities that make a difference.
>
> —Thom Rainer and Eric Geiger, *Simple Church*

to a role that coordinated all the work of age-group ministry. Then together the staff began to work on the direction they wanted to go in ministry.

In reviewing what they were doing with children and students, they realized that the average child or student in their church receives about forty hours a year of Bible study in their church, hardly enough to form the disciples they wanted kids to become. They also realized that parents have approximately three thousand hours a year with their kids when they are not at school or church or involved in some other activity. If the church partnered with parents and encouraged parents to devote some time to discipleship, the potential for growth in kids was much greater.

The next step wasn't to look at the ministry plan. The Brentwood staff decided that before they could determine what they would do in ministry, they wanted to set goals. They asked these questions: "What characteristics do we want to see in kids who grow up participating in the age-group ministries of Brentwood Baptist Church? And then, based on those characteristics, what will we need to do to help them acquire those traits?" They created a document they call "Parenting Six. Seven." The document describes six characteristics followed by seven ministry venues/strategies/opportunities the church will use to help kids develop those strategies.

> Parents who have a plan, overall, have more positive parenting experiences.
>
> —LifeWay Research

The basis for the "Parenting Six. Seven" document is Deuteronomy 6:4–9 (NIV): "Hear, O Israel: The LORD our God, the LORD is one. Love the LORD your God with all your heart and with all your soul and with all your strength. These commandments that I give you today are to be upon your hearts. Impress them on your children. Talk about them when you sit at home and when you walk along the road, when you lie down and when you get up. Tie them as symbols on your hands and bind them on your foreheads. Write them on the doorframes of your houses and on your gates." The document's focus is on verse 7: "Impress them on your children. Talk about them when you sit at home and when you walk along the road, when you lie down and when you get up." Jay says they like the New International Version translation for these verses because of the word *impress*, which means "to carve out." They want "to carve out" kids who are in the shape of Jesus Christ.

Six characteristics of a child/student who loves God with all their heart, soul, and strength:

1. Loves God as a way of life (worship) (see Rom. 12:1–2)
2. Loves others as a way of life (service) (see Mark 10:45)
3. Loves the church and understands his/her role in the body of Christ (community) (see Eph. 4:4–7)
4. Loves the Bible and can handle it properly as the authority and foundation for life (Scripture) (see 2 Tim. 3:15–17)
5. Loves to share God's story (the gospel) and their story (testimony) and is ready to engage others in their story (evangelism) (see Rom. 10:14–15)
6. Loves to grow closer to God through personal spiritual disciplines such as prayer and personal Bible study (discipleship) (see 1 Tim. 4:7–12)

Seven ministry venues/strategies/opportunities that will partner with parents to "impress" (constantly reinforce) these six characteristics:

1. Synchronize our ministry efforts around this master plan to build faith and character in our sons and daughters.
2. Communicate this expectation and plan clearly to parents.
3. Develop a resource guide that suggests to parents recommended resources for family devotions and specific family issues.
4. Connect our teaching ministries to the home.
5. Provide catalyst venues that introduce parents to "Parenting Six. Seven."

6. Partner with the missions department to provide family-friendly mission venues.

7. Partner with the worship team to focus on intergenerational and family worship gatherings.

The seven strategies have details that include critical assumptions, areas of impact, and specific tasks. For example, to accomplish strategy 6, "Partner with the missions department to provide family-friendly mission venues," the church has a goal by next year to have fifty family-oriented missions experiences and trips based on Acts 1:8, with some missions opportunities local, some national, and some international. One of the reasons they are doing this is that when they have asked adults what they remember about their youth ministry years, they may remember having a lot of fun, but they also recall powerful experiences of ministry and missions. These were strongest when they worked alongside their parents.

While partnering with parents, Brentwood's age-group ministers are not abandoning their specific ministries with each age group. Since 40 percent of the children and students at Brentwood attend without their parents, the church takes seriously its role of spiritual formation with this group of kids. Age-group ministers also understand that by ministering with each age group they are reinforcing the parents' "as you go" discipleship.

> We overestimate tomorrow. We underestimate today. The truth is that the most important day you will experience is today.
>
> —Author John Maxwell

The goal of all the age-group ministers is to offer a consistent approach to education and discipleship in three critical parts of their ministry to kids: (1) content, (2) context, and (3) catalyst. (1) The content is based on God's Word, the Bible. (2) The context is the church's ministries with each age group. (3) Age-group ministers recognize that the primary catalyst of spiritual formation is a kid's parents. The church is partnering with parents to be the catalyst for disciple-making.

Part of being the catalyst means communicating with parents so that parents know what the church is teaching and so church and parents work together. Teachers can provide parents questions from each Sunday's Bible study to facilitate discussion with their kids about the lesson. Being the catalyst also means training leaders and continuing to equip children and students.

As they disciple kids and parents together, the goal is to help people live different lives, lives set apart as missional parents. As believers become more Christlike, they will be an example to others. And when

> Simple church leaders check the fit. Before a new ministry is launched, they ensure it is a viable part of the simple ministry process. They clarify specifically how the new ministry will move people through the process. And they ensure that the leaders of the new ministry understand how the ministry is part of the big picture.
>
> —Thom Rainer and Eric Geiger, *Simple Church*

people see the difference in their lives and ask about it, they can follow Peter's admonition to "always be ready to give a defense to anyone who asks you for a reason for the hope that is in you (1 Pet. 3:15).[3]

Biblical Truth

Jesus used this parenting example in the parable of the two sons to teach about His favorite subject, the kingdom of God:

"But what do you think? A man had two sons. He went to the first and said, 'My son, go, work in the vineyard today.'

"He answered, 'I don't want to!' Yet later he changed his mind and went. Then the man went to the other and said the same thing.

"'I will, sir' he answered. But he didn't go.

"Which of the two did his father's will?"

"The first," they said.

Jesus said to them, "I assure you: Tax collectors and prostitutes are entering the kingdom of God before you! For John came to you in the way of righteousness, and you didn't believe him. Tax collectors and prostitutes did believe him, but you, when you saw it, didn't even change your minds then and believe him." (Matt. 21:28–32)

Jesus was using this parable specifically because He was speaking to church leaders in the temple. He condemned the chief priests and elders of the people for their lack of belief in John's message of repentance.

As we think about our role in church, it is worth another look at Jesus' question: "Which of the two did his father's will?" In relation to our church, are we content when young people give the right answers in church or are polite enough to say, "Sir?" Or are we really preparing them to make right choices when they are on their own? If we are honest, we have to admit we do not always have the end in mind.

The Prayer Focus

God, our Loving Father, You know the plans You have for the children You've given us even before they are born. We know that Your plans are good. Guide us as parents and church members to teach our children to plan to walk in Your ways. Thank You for trusting us to raise the children You have given us. Lead us always to trust You to meet the needs of our family. In the name of the One who taught us to pray, our Savior Jesus Christ, amen.

Parent Adventures

1. Think of a family with similar age children as yours and plan ways you can help each other begin letting go. For example, take turns watching each others' kids so the parents can have a date night. Or plan those first sleepovers at each others' houses, where you are well aware of and comfortable with the home environment.

2. Plan a relaxed family night. Depending on the weather, go outside, lie on your backs and look at the stars, or stay inside and build a fire in the fireplace, or enjoy a carpet picnic. Then spend some time dreaming. Let each family member share some goals, hopes, and dreams. Encourage one another. How can you help make some of those dreams come true?

3. Deuteronomy 6:6–7 instructs parents to talk with children as they go. Parents today do a lot of going. Plan important topics to talk about with your child as you go.

QUESTIONS FOR DISCUSSION

1. Share ways God has shown you to begin letting go. Your obedience or change of perspective can be an encouragement to other parents.

2. List things your church does already to help parents and children with milestones and transitions.

3. What fears did you have when you were the age your children are now? What fears do your children have? How can

you help your church plan tangible ways to assist children with those fears? What does the Bible say about fears (see Josh. 1:9; Ps. 56; 2 Tim. 1:7)? What does it say about the fears of your children?

4. What are ways that your church allows, or better yet, encourages children or students to participate in ministry? Are there some additional ways that you could begin to let go and let them serve?

Chapter 9

A Yes Church

You will know the truth, and the truth will set you free.

—JOHN 8:32

Churches, like homes, can be "yes" places for children and teenagers. "Yes, you may read a book instead of building a block home," is affirming to preschoolers. "Yes, you can help bake cookies to show our appreciation to law enforcement officers and fire fighters" teaches children to appreciate community leaders. "Yes, you can lead in worship and go on a mission trip," teaches teenagers to minister rather than simply to receive ministry.

In researching multi-site churches for my (Scott's) book *Multi-Site Churches: Guidance for the Movement's Next Generation,* I ran across several churches that exemplify what a yes church looks like. Pastor Nathan Lewis describes Evergreen Presbyterian in Beaverton, Oregon: "We are missions minded. We are committed with our dollars and our strategy to multiply congregations for worship." In addition to this proactive, missional mind-set, Nathan points out that they are "genuinely hospitable and welcoming." This willingness to accept others is reflected in a congregation that includes people of all economic levels.

A key event in the life of Evergreen Presbyterian involved several families in the church who had yes homes. These families had moved to Newberg, about 30 minutes from Beaverton, but continued to commute that distance each week for church. Their children started playing water polo at the Newberg club. If the parents had stopped saying yes at this point, there would be no story of kingdom impact.

Instead, when their boys asked, one of the families agreed to open their home on Friday night for the club to socialize. God began to work among these teenage friends, and two boys asked if they could have a Bible study when they got together on Friday nights. The family said yes, and soon those two boys professed faith in Christ and were asking to go to Evergreen to participate in the youth group. The boys' families were interested enough to join them.

Knowing that such a long commute was not conducive for these new families to get involved, the members petitioned the session of elders to do something for these families in the Newberg area. The session responded, and on October 2, 2005, Evergreen became a multi-site church. Nathan Lewis began preaching at Beaverton at 9:00 a.m. and at Newberg at 11:00 a.m. each Sunday. By Christmas 2005, he had baptized twenty-eight people, including teenagers from the water polo team, their parents, and their extended families. The combination of a yes home that was open to their boys' ideas and a yes church that was willing to move when they saw God at work has had an eternal impact.

Are American Homes Free?

Clearly, Christian yes homes can make a difference, but how common are they? Findings from the LifeWay Research parent survey reveal that many homes need to experience the freedom of yes, and even more need to experience the truth that can set them free eternally. First, note these statistics showing that up to half of American parents admit the tone of their home needs improvement:

- More than two-thirds of parents describe their home as positive and supportive.
- More than one-fourth of the parents surveyed do not describe their home as positive and supportive.
- Half of the parents describe their home as optimistic.
- Only 3 percent of the parents surveyed consider their home pessimistic.

As parents seek to favor saying yes and minimize saying no, how do you determine where this line should be? The Word of God provides this standard. The Holy Spirit guides into all truth. Determining when we might say no begins with applying these truths. Often the decisions that don't challenge a truth may require a "wait" response rather than a no. For example, children tend to be extremely creative at bedtime. Foregoing sleep for most of their ideas is not wise, but planning to try their ideas the next day is a form of saying yes.

Although a majority of parents' descriptions of their homes were positive, many parents were unwilling to say that some of these positive descriptions fit their home. For example, 61 percent were not willing to call their home "peaceful," and 43 percent were unwilling to say that it's "joyful."

Despite the unchanging value of the truth in God's Word, the majority of American parents have not embraced the Bible for what

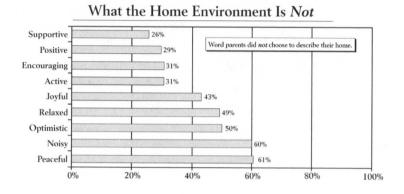

Figure 1. What the Home Environment Is *Not*

it is. This leads to roughly half of parents not entrusting their eternity to Jesus Christ. The following statistics on American parents' faith and beliefs lend perspective on what needs to change for many parents:

- A minority (42 percent) strongly agree that the Bible is the written Word of God and is totally accurate in all that it teaches.
- A majority (57 percent) strongly agree that they have made a personal commitment to Jesus Christ that is important in their lives today.
- Less than half of parents in America believe they will go to heaven because they "have accepted Jesus Christ as their Savior."

Churches Can Help Parents Teach the Truth

Parents can more easily have a yes home if they have a plan for parenting that includes letting go and setting boundaries based on

God's Word as a guide for living. Children and teenagers who grow up in such a home then learn what is required for parents to say yes. For example, a teenager asks to go to a party. He or she knows that parents will not say yes to a party where they have not met the parents. The teenager knows that the following questions will be asked: Whose house? Will the parents be at home? Who will be there? What are the plans for the party? Students who plan in advance for their parents to meet the host family of an upcoming party are more likely to get a yes when they ask to go to a party at that home.

Clara Mae Van Brink—a psychiatric nurse; retired preschool minister from Peachtree Corners Baptist Church in Norcross, Georgia; writer; and conference leader—says that providing conferences for parents about setting boundaries is just one of many ways to help parents. And setting boundaries that children grow up understanding actually creates a yes home, not a no home, because children know in advance how to get a yes answer.[1]

Knowing God's Plan. In fact, the whole concept of having a yes home can be tied to knowing and understanding God's guidelines for living, and that is where parents and the church can partner in training children for a yes environment. James R. Estep Jr., a professor of Christian education at Lincoln Christian Seminary in Illinois, affirms the essential role of God's Word in the foundation for every family and for parents and churches partnering in faith formation. He explains that this concept is as simple as understanding

> The Bible is the written Word of God and is totally accurate in all that it teaches.
>
> - 42 percent of parents agree strongly.
> - 28 percent agree somewhat.
> - 20 percent disagree somewhat.
> - 10 percent disagree strongly.

"Jesus loves me! This I know, for the Bible tells me so."[2] And it's as ancient as the Ten Commandments.[3]

Our foundational Bible text for this book, the Shema, found in Deuteronomy 6, is part of God's law given to Moses by God. Those instructions tell what will be taught, the Bible; who will be taught, children; and by whom, parents. And how are parents to learn? In the Old Testament, they were to be taught by the priests. In the New Testament, believers learned from the apostles teaching in Jerusalem (Acts 2:42) and in other cities where they traveled, such as Ephesus (Acts 19:9–10).

About this teaching process, Estep writes:

> Early in Israel's history as a nation, educational responsibility was placed primarily on the family. Both parents were to be involved in the instruction of their children (Prov. 1:8), as well as other family members, making education in the family an intergenerational matter (Deut. 4:9–11; 11:19–20; Exod. 12:26–27). Perhaps the most telling passage in this regard is Psalm 78, where God's interventions on Israel's behalf are recounted with the exhortation for parents to recount these events to the children. Christian education has always included the passing down of the history and traditions of the faith community, so our faith becomes an intergenerational affair. . . .

Churches who see people turning to follow Jesus Christ often make a point of sharing these stories of God's life-changing work in a worship service or when they are baptized. Technology also enables churches to tell the story of God's work in new and exciting ways. Many churches now use video or blog entries on the church Web site to retell significant events in the church's life and in individuals' lives.

—LifeWay Research

However, parents alone were not the teachers of the faith community. Priests received formal education and provided instruction to the community. . . . The priests used the law in their instruction. . . . The priesthood represented the establishment of the first permanent group of teachers in Israel *outside* the family.[4]

Estep speaks not only to who did the teaching but also to what was taught and why:

> The purpose of instruction was also to lead someone to make a personal commitment and greater maturity. In the Old Testament the nation of Israel received instruction and then had to choose between faithfulness and rejection of God. . . . Even the resident "alien" was to participate regularly in the community's instruction. . . .
>
> Perhaps even more evident is the Great Commission of the New Testament (Matt. 28:18–20). Jesus' commission to His disciples to continue His disciple-making endeavors explicitly included teaching. Christian education must maintain the focus on making disciples of Christ, which does not simply end with conversion but requires continual instruction for maturing in the faith.[5]

All of this is foundational to having a yes home. When the foundation is secure, parents are free to say yes. Note, too, that instruction is for both followers of Christ and for those who are identified as aliens, foreigners, Gentiles, or unbelievers.

Knowing What to Teach Your Children. If the foundation of a yes home is a solid understanding of God's Word and biblical truths, some parents may be wondering just what those truths are and how they can teach them to their children. Most parents know about the "dos" and the "do nots" of the Ten Commandments, but laying a foundation for children first to become believers and then to become maturing disciples means a far greater understanding than the Ten Commandments. If you

> I can answer the one who taunts me,
> for I trust in Your word.
> Never take the word of truth from my mouth,
> for I hope in Your judgments.
> I will always keep Your law,
> forever and ever.
> I will walk freely in an open place
> because I seek Your precepts.
> I will speak of Your decrees before kings
> and not be ashamed.
> I delight in Your commands,
> which I love.
> I will lift up my hands to Your commands,
> which I love,
> and will meditate on Your statutes.
>
> —Psalm 119:42–48

look at our selected Scripture for this book, Deuteronomy 6:5–7, you might be wondering what exactly are the words parents should be teaching to their children.

Parents can learn a lot about age-appropriate biblical concepts they can discuss with their kids by being familiar with the curriculum their children are using in Sunday school, children's worship, Vacation Bible School, and other church activities. Good curriculum will teach biblical concepts appropriate for the child. The complexity increases at different levels as children move from birth through preteens.

KyAnne Weaver, children's and family life director at Pocono Community Church, said, "I tell my volunteers, 'We are a little like a soup kitchen on Sunday morning because we can feed the kids, but they are going to go home through the week. If their parents are not backing up what we are teaching and we are not working together, they are not being fed during the week.'

"We need to keep ministering on Sundays, but we have got to work together with the families and hopefully have what we are teaching reinforced at home. And we want to reinforce what parents are teaching as well. We are here to serve the family."

KyAnne's primary focus in helping parents is driven by her recognition that most parents need help getting to

> What a child doesn't receive, he can seldom later give.
> —Author P. D. James

know the Word of God. "We can't impress on them what we do not know ourselves. For this reason parents feel intimidated about having family devotions or even teaching their children and training them spiritually. To help build up families, I write devotions every week to go with our lesson."

As parents pick up their children on Sunday, KyAnne provides them with a devotional card. On one side it tells what the children did that day at church and has the memory verse. On the other side she provides five short devotions for Monday through Friday that she has written. They typically include a statement or a question and a couple of verses. "If the children's lesson Sunday was on overcoming fear, Monday's devotion would say, 'In the car on the way to school or the ball game, tell your kids about a time when you were afraid when you were their age. And when you have time today, read this Scripture together.'

"It's funny because I really thought my 'churchy' families would latch onto this idea and be all excited, but without fail it is my single parents who say, 'Thank you! We do these every night. I don't know what else to do, but we do these. I didn't know where else to go.'"

As children grow, their ability to understand and apply biblical truths increases. They can understand their need for accepting Christ as Savior and making Him Lord. Then they can apply what they learn to how they live; they can begin to make their faith known to others. Scott Stevens, LifeWay director of student ministry, said, "The foundation of a strategy for student development is expressed in Luke 2:52: 'And Jesus increased in wisdom and stature, and in favor with God and with people' and in the Sermon on the Mount. The strategy revolves around three words: *know*—upward development, 'Jesus increased . . . in favor with God'; *own*—inward development, 'Jesus increased in wisdom and stature'; and *known*—outward development, 'Jesus increased . . . in favor with . . . people.' *Know* focuses on growth in lordship and discipleship; *own* focuses on growth in character and discernment; and *known* focuses on relationships and influence. The goal is for students to *know* God, *own* their faith, and to make their faith *known*."[6]

> You have made a personal commitment to Jesus Christ that is still important in your life today.
> - 57 percent of parents agree strongly.
> - 26 percent agree somewhat.
> - 10 percent disagree somewhat.
> - 8 percent disagree strongly.

Knowing How to Teach Children. We've established from research that parents overwhelming agree that their children's spiritual formation is their responsibility, and we've looked at Scripture and the work of Christian educators to see how parents are taught. However parents are often gun-shy about passing along these truths. Two seminary doctoral students chose as their final project to follow up with parents about the spiritual formation of their children.

"When these students talked with the parents in their respective churches, they found that parents did not know how to teach their children spiritual truths."[7]

When you talk about parents' setting boundaries, disciplining their children, or other issues, talk first about the parents' relationships with each other and the examples they set for their children.

A number of churches are finding ways to disciple parents in order to disciple children and students. The time to begin this process with parents is early in the life of the child. In fact, some churches begin by offering parenting classes even before the baby is born.

Along with practical information from medical experts about caring for a newborn, church leaders can share ideas about how the church will partner with parents in the parents' role of discipling their children.

Here are practical things many churches already do to reinforce a yes approach as biblical truths are taught:

Preschool. Each week preschoolers are given age-appropriate centers in their classroom among which they can choose; teachers are guided in how to use the activity in the center to reinforce the biblical truth being taught that week.

Children. During weekly children's programs children are given choices of activities that help with their understanding or application of the biblical truth.

Preteens. Weekly Bible study is not something the teacher "does." Preteens themselves examine Scripture, act out applications, and participate in discussion.

Teenagers. Throughout a church's student activities and many church activities, individual students are given responsibility. They can be seen on the welcoming team, handing out worship guides, playing instruments in a praise band or orchestra, acting on a drama team, singing in a choir, teaching younger children, participating in servant evangelism, and more.

> "Everything is permissible," but not everything is helpful.
> "Everything is permissible," but not everything builds up.
>
> —1 Corinthians 10:23

In addition to equipping parents to teach children, the church can provide ways for parents and children to experience the purpose and work of the church together.

Pocono Community Church has conducted activities that they called "Pray It Forward" in which grade-school children and their parents participate together. Children's and family life director KyAnne Weaver explained, "We are going to pray, but we are also going to put feet to our faith and go serve. Then because they are children, we give them something fun."

One month on a Saturday morning, they prayed for a Bible camp near them. They then went to the camp and raked leaves and finished with a fun hayride and wiener roast. Another month they prayed for senior-care facilities and the people in them and then did something for them. The church has created an opportunity for parents and children to serve together.

Centerpoint Church in Colton, California, has a one-hour family service each Wednesday night called FamilyStuf. Kids (pre-k through sixth grade) and their parents worship together and focus on one of God's virtues each month. The worship includes upbeat music, fun teaching, and great dramas and seeks to transform parents, family conversation, and families into all God wants them to be.

Another way some churches are finding ways to help parents know what to teach and how to teach it is by discipling parents and teenagers at the same time. They journey together in spiritual formation. First Baptist Church of Hendersonville, Tennessee, provides a good example. Dave Paxton is director of their student ministry. He explained how their ministry, RipCord, is helping both parents and students grow as disciples.

Dave explained the title of the ministry, RipCord:

> Imagine yourself at ten thousand feet in an airplane, getting ready to jump, complete with parachute, helmet, and boots. Just as the plane lines up for final approach to the drop zone, the pilot calls out, "Jump run!" The instructor looks at you and says, "OK . . . there are eight things you need to know before you make this jump!" Would you be very motivated to listen to those eight things? Would they seem very important to you at the time? Would they be more important given the situation than they might be in a classroom setting somewhere?
>
> Each year students from First Baptist graduate from high school and our student ministry and head into an uncertain future. We believe there are eight foundational truths they need to grasp before "jumping" into the world of college and a career. Understanding that the parent is the number one influencer in the faith development of a teenager, we realized that perhaps, in the past, we had been approaching discipleship in the wrong way.[8]

Although the ministry is only eighteen months old and had a difficult start, Dave believes it is already meeting needs and will continue to grow. Parents who have walked the journey with their teenagers are enlisted to serve as mentors to other parents to answer questions and to encourage them throughout the discipleship process.

The student leaders at First Hendersonville have a goal of making the parents the heroes rather than setting up the youth minister or lay leaders in student ministry to be the heroes. Student ministry realized that this would not be an automatic attraction for all students and their parents. Some parents would feel inadequate. Some students wouldn't want their parents "teaching" them. They've developed a set of frequently asked questions to help both students and parents deal with some of their reservations. For example:

> **What if my teen says they do not want me teaching them?**
> That will be an often heard comment. A suggested response
> is, "I agree. I am not going to teach you. We are going
> through this together and will discuss what we learned.
> I am learning this with you. Sometimes you might even
> teach ME something you discovered." (Remember, the goal
> is to lead them to discover spiritual truths. It's okay if you
> don't immediately get the credit.)[9]

Dave says that the single biggest complaint he gets now from teenagers enrolled in the ministry is that they don't like the break between semesters. They'd like to be having this regular study time with mom and/or dad all the time. Parents are also pleased. One parent wrote:

> Dave, I just wanted to drop you a line to tell you that
> RipCord is transforming our daughter's spiritual life. We
> have always been a family who prays together and does our
> own personal studies, but RipCord has taken Kendall to a
> new level. She has Scripture cards posted throughout her
> area at home. Over her desk is always the memory verse
> for the week. She has a sign that she has created that says,
> "Remember to spend time with God today. What's
> 5 minutes for Him when He has given eternity to you?"
> The God-sized challenges have been so inspirational. She

has befriended a boy in her class who is a troublemaker. No
one likes him. He sits by himself at lunch; and when others
are around him, they tease and ridicule him. Kendall has
taken him under her wing, with lots of adversity from her
fellow classmates. She has reached out to him in Christian
love, and this boy is amazed that someone cares about him.
One of her friends began to tease her and asked Kendall if
she liked him as a boyfriend. Kendall told her friend that
she did not like him in that respect, but her RipCord Bible
study encouraged embracing someone who was hurting and
needed Christ's love. Her friend responded: "Cool!" This is
my shy child who has stepped up to the plate where God is
concerned.

She is also seeking out Scripture, outside of the study,
to encourage her. She is faced with so much with the world
and identity and self-worth. She has a Scripture card on her
bathroom mirror to remind her that "the King is enthralled
with your beauty" so as she struggles with not feeling
beautiful, God's Word reminds her every day of how lovely
she is to Him. She has implemented these techniques on her
own. God has laid these things on her heart. She will stay
up extra late to make sure she has done her Bible study. The
other night she had a big test to study for and she insisted
on doing her Bible study first, no matter how late she would
be up studying. She holds me accountable and reminds me
about putting my Bible study before my chores. Working
together with her has taken each of us to a new spiritual
connection. God is doing amazing things in her life.

I found a letter of encouragement she had written to a
girl in her class who is struggling with her identity. Her letter
was amazing, filled with God-based words and Scripture.
I am so thankful for RipCord and the difference it is
making in her life. Your efforts are paying off with my teen.

Parents and students who grow as disciples together will grow into mature, missional believers with a Christian worldview. Like the teen described in the mother's e-mail to Dave Paxton, both teenage and adult disciples will begin applying biblical truths to their daily lives. And an environment like that produces yes homes, homes where parents are more often able to say yes to their children because of a mutual understanding of biblical barriers and a home where believers of all ages say yes to God.

> His intent was that now, through the church, the manifold wisdom of God should be made known.
>
> —Ephesians 3:10 NIV

The Prayer Focus

Father, God, we know that all our yeses are found in You. Thank You for all the ways You have provided for our families. Thank You for Your Word that gives us direction and freedom. Thank You for Your discipline as we seek to grow as Your disciples. Show us ways to help our children find their yes in You. In the name of our Savior who said yes and gave Himself to die that we might live, we pray. Amen.

Parent Adventures

1. Share ideas with other parents about ways they can have a yes home.
2. Work with age-group ministers or leaders in your church to plan a parenting seminar on creative discipline with ideas for having a yes home. If your church is small, you may want to partner with another church to invite a Christian counselor to lead this session.

3. List significant things God has done in your life and your family's life. Be prepared to follow the example in Psalm 78 and share this with your children, other parents, and other children you know at church.

QUESTIONS FOR DISCUSSION

1. List ways your church says yes to preschoolers, children, and teenagers. Then brainstorm new ideas for saying yes. Choose one or two for each age group that can move from ideas to actions.
2. Paul said that real freedom comes in obeying God (Gal. 5). Share biblical truths you want your children to know and obey. Discuss with age-group leaders how and when these are being taught or will be taught. Share ideas to emphasize biblical truths at home and at church at the same time.
3. Talk about the words *disciple* and *discipline*. Why does one sound positive and one sound negative? How can parents make discipline a yes word?

Chapter 10

Facilitating Conversation

*I will speak mysteries from the past—things we have heard
and known and that our fathers have passed down to us.
We must not hide them from their children, but must tell a
future generation the praises of the LORD, His might, and
the wonderful works He has performed.*

—PSALM 78:2–4

We've got it all wrong. Sundays are *not* the big game day.
They're the practice before the big game. The big game
happens when we sit at home, eat dinner together, travel
on the road, talk to clients, listen to our teachers at school, chat at
the water cooler, communicate on the Web, text and talk on the
cell phone, and read the mail. That's where life is lived, and that's
where I need help showing my kids our God is all we need, that He's
just as real, just as cool, just as awesome, and just as loving now as

He was in that Bible story they learned about in Sunday school."
Donny Rockwell, a parent from Oklahoma, expresses the need for
good communication "as we go." Conversations about our walk
with Jesus should be natural and frequent in our daily comings and
goings. The church can help parents have those kinds of conversations with their kids. That's what this chapter is all about.

Churches with age-group leaders and ministers who spend
time listening to children and teenagers and encouraging them to
ask questions are helping them think about their relationships with
God and with others. Churches that help parents have faith-based
conversations with their children multiply the benefits children get
at church because, as you know well by now, parents are not only
responsible for their children's spiritual formation and development;
they are also the greatest influence on their children's lives.

LifeWay Research can help us get a clear picture of where parents in the United States see themselves and their families in this
important area of communication. Only 17 percent said the quality
of communication among family members is excellent while most
(68 percent) called it either good or very good.

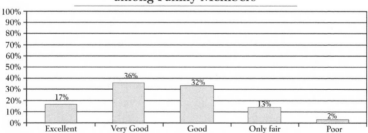

Figure 1. Rating the Quality of Communication among Family
Members

Here are some additional research findings from the parenting survey:

- Eight out of ten parents say "I love you" to their children every day.
- Almost all parents say "You can do this" and "I'm proud of you" once a month or more, but three out of ten also say "I'm disappointed in you" that frequently.
- Seven out of ten parents indicate that communication is equally likely to be initiated by them or their children.
- The older the children, the *less* likely they are to hear daily that their parents are proud of them, love them, or that they are important.
- Higher income parents are *less* likely than others to say "I'm proud of you," or to indicate they believe in their child or that their child is important on a daily basis.
- Fathers are *less* likely than mothers to say to their children on a daily basis: "I believe in you," "You can do this," "I'm proud of you," or "You're important."

Regarding communication about faith or religion, the survey indicated that half of American families at least monthly pray together, have a family meeting, or attend religious services

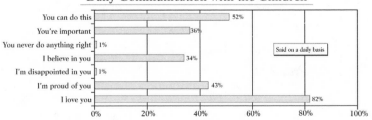

Figure 2. Daily Communication with the Children

together. In contrast, only 31 percent of families do religious studies or devotionals together.

How Churches Are Responding

Church leaders can encourage one-on-one conversations between children or students and parents about faith issues and other important matters that lead to greater heart connections and an appreciation of each other's walk with Christ. Richard Ross, professor of student ministry at Southwestern Baptist Theological Seminary, developed one such resource, *30 Days: Turning the Hearts of Parents and Teenagers Toward Each Other*. Here's how Richard describes this resource:

> Each evening a parent and teenager go to a room with a closed door and pull chairs near each other. They light a candle and turn off the other lights. They break the seal on the *30 Days* envelope for that night. For the first time they see the five cards for that evening. Some cards go to the teenager and some go to the parent. By following the instructions on the cards, the parent and teenager say and do those things that have the most powerful potential to turn their hearts toward each other.
>
> Also, each evening they find a fresh way to pray together. Many thousands of families have seen dramatic changes in relationships through this experience. (For more information, go to www.josiahpress.com.)[1]

Start with Preschoolers

Beth Tolar, a preschool minister in West Columbia, South Carolina, provides seminars for parents about a variety of topics including: "How to Talk with Your Child about Sex," "How to Share Your Faith," and "How to Teach Preschoolers." All of these seminars encourage conversation between preschoolers and parents. Beth says, "During the sex conference we stressed the importance of having ongoing conversations with your child about various things so that when difficult topics—or should I say uncomfortable topics—arise, parents have a foundation of conversations and they are more at ease. If they are not at ease, they should be honest about their feelings and share them with their child."

When they give children Bibles, they give them the translation they use in Sunday school so that children hear the same words at church and at home. Sunday school leaders also provide take-home information to give parents ideas for talking with their children about what they did during Sunday school beyond, "What did you do in Sunday school today?" Equipped with specific questions, parents can have better conversations and reinforce the learning throughout the week.

Beth points out that conversation helps build relationships, and children are hungry for a relationship with their parents. She says: "Parents need to be a role model for their child. They need to see them reading their Bible, praying, and worshipping. Children long for relationship, and they need to see their parents having a

---

Words of affection and endearment, words of praise and encouragement, words that give positive guidance all say, "I care about you." Such words are like a gentle, warm rain falling on the soul; they nurture the child's inner sense of worth and security. Even though such words are quickly said, they are not soon forgotten. A child reaps the benefits of affirming words for a lifetime.

—Gary Chapman and Ross Campbell,
The Five Love Languages of Children

relationship with Jesus. We in the church need to remember that the Christian faith is based on a relationship.[2]

Electronic Communication in a Postmodern Age

After twelve years as youth minister, Bill Newton's church in Lonoke, Arkansas, asked him to make the transition to youth and children's minister. One of his goals is to facilitate communication between parents and children from birth until parents send kids off to college or to work. One of the ways he does this is with a parents' e-mail newsletter to keep parents informed. Parents receive the newsletter on Wednesday telling them what their kids will be studying in Sunday school the following Sunday along with questions and ideas to guide parents in talking with their kids about Bible study and discipleship both before and after the students experience the Bible study at church. The ideas are age graded and specific to the lesson. For example, when young children are learning about creation at church, suggestions might include a parent-child nature walk with both parent and child pointing out things that God made. The nature walk becomes a teachable moment that reinforces the Bible concept.

The newsletter includes information beyond the Sunday school. The newsletter also outlines what students will be studying on Wednesday nights and suggests questions for Thursday morning breakfast to aid conversation and to reinforce the Bible truth from the night before. Bill says he includes information about culture for students: "Culture is a big deal for students. So I give parents links to Web sites to help them deal with issues in the home about culture. I also include some quotes that may be fun with just a grain of truth in them. The newsletter needs to be entertaining too."

Here are some excerpts from one week of Bill's e-newsletter that help parents talk with their kids:

Youth Wednesday Night

Each night I emphasize The ONE Thing (a thought) I want them to walk away with. Below is The ONE Thing for Wednesday night along with the discussion questions.

The Hope in Temptation (1 Corinthians 10:1–13)

The ONE Thing: Temptation is never so overwhelming that we can't resist it.

1. What's your first reaction to the promise in verse 13? What kind of encouragement does that bring you?

2. What do you think are the implications/results of a verse like this when put in the context of spiritual warfare we've been talking about?

3. How can the previous weapons we've discussed (love, prayer, the Word, fasting) "provide a way out"?

4. What would happen if you memorized this one verse and every time you felt tempted to the point you can't resist the temptation you quoted this verse? How do you think that would help/encourage you? (Doing this would be an example of using the Word as a weapon and responding to temptation just as Jesus did in Matthew 4.)

Ideas for How to Use This E-Newsletter

Launch discussions with your children/youth over Sunday dinner and/or as you travel to school, ball practice, etc.

Kicking It Off—Getting the conversation started is sometimes the hardest part. It's best to use open-ended questions that lead to discussion instead of closed questions that only require a yes or no answer. Here are some good open-ended questions to get you started:

- What did you learn/talk about in Sunday school?
- What was the point of the lesson?

- What do you think about that principle/lesson/idea?
- How does that principle/lesson/idea apply to everyday life?
- How can you apply this to your day-to-day life?

Be sure to follow up these questions after a few days to see if/how your children are applying what they learned. Encouragement and accountability are great things to teach your children. Knowledge is useless if it's not used.

Keep the Lessons Handy—Copy and paste the lesson information you need from this newsletter into a program such as Word and print out that part of the newsletter that relates to the age groups of your children. Place it somewhere you can see and use it such as the fridge, mirror, or dashboard of your vehicle.

The feedback Bill is getting is that this strategy is working. Parents say they are using the newsletter to launch conversations with their kids at least occasionally if not every week. Here's one response Bill received from a parent:

Bro. Bill,

I think the newsletter is extremely helpful. Because of the times we are in, we find ourselves scrounging for every minute to squeeze as much stuff in as we can for our kids. The newsletter not only allows me to know what my kids are going to be talking about in Sunday school and Kid's Church but also allows me to ask questions at home to reinforce what is taught.

When you ask your child a specific question about what they learned in Sunday school, they realize that you are aware of their walk with Christ. This reinforces the bond between God and our children and lets them know how important we find this walk to be.

By having this weekly e-mail, I am able to read this at my convenience and keep up with the church activities as well as what my children are learning. I think it is a great tool for any parent!

Bill is pleased with that as a start. He hopes it will continue to build momentum in the homes for good communication.

In 2007, LifeWay Research conducted a study of young adults that revealed a very strong connection between teenagers' relationships with adults at church and their likelihood to stay in church. The study was conducted among young adults who had attended a Protestant church for at least a year in high school. Overall, 70 percent of those over age twenty-two indicated they had stopped attending church regularly for at least a year between ages eighteen and twenty-two. Now, watch the stair-step difference that relationships with adults make.

In their book *Essential Church*, Thom and Sam Rainer summarize the implications for church leaders. "The great news about this

The Impact of Adults at Church Investing in Teens

How many adults from church do you feel made a significant investment in you personally and spiritually between the ages of fifteen and eighteen? Young adults who attended a Protestant church regularly for at least a year in high school indicate:

Number of Adults Who Invested in Their Life Between Ages Fifteen and Eighteen	Percent Who Dropped Out*
None	89 percent
1	76 percent
2	68 percent
3 or 4	59 percent
5 or 6	57 percent
7 or more	50 percent

* Stopped attending church regularly for at least a year between ages 18 and 22

Figure 3. The Impact of Adults at Church Investing in Teens

research is the simplicity of keeping students. . . . No complicated process. No cookie-cutter formula. No huge program. No expensive resources. Just start encouraging adults and teens to mix with one another through existing church events. That's it."[3]

As parents, we circulate with other parents in our church as well as their children. We have opportunities every week to make a direct investment in a child's life and future outlook on the church by caring enough to take an interest in them. We also can begin to recognize ways in which we can encourage parents to master productive talk systems with their kids.

Bill Newton is also concerned about kids going off to college and suddenly not having strong faith-based ties. The church now offers an eight-week study group for students and parents to handle the transition to college. The information about these sessions went to the parents, inviting them to come and bring their students. Bill's thinking was that students will stay in touch with their families while they will only rarely communicate with church leaders. In the sessions they are addressing things like money, dating, partying, and credit cards. In the students' presence they are suggesting ways for parents to follow up with their students and to keep them accountable.

Bill sums up his philosophy with this: "Kids are postmodern, asking questions. Parents often were discouraged from asking questions when they were kids. Parents may have accepted their faith without asking a lot of questions. When their children ask some really tough questions about faith and discipleship, parents often don't know how to respond. They don't have the answers. Our goal is to equip parents to talk with their kids and to be able to answer their questions. This begins when children are baptized. They study a book and learn together." [4]

First Baptist Lewisville, Texas, has another approach. All the age-group ministers and leaders have made a commitment to communicate with parents what their children are learning at church. They do this in different ways. For example, the student ministry created a communication called Scoop, which contains questions for parents to talk with their teenagers about what happened on Sunday morning. The questions are written to help parents and students have spiritual conversations and for them to become a normal part of parent-teenager conversation.[5]

Churches facilitate parent-child conversation in other ways:

- Some use curriculum that includes take-home pieces for parents or conversation starters for parents.
- North Point Community Church in Alpharetta, Georgia, sends postcards to parents with tips for connecting with Bible truths children have learned that week at church.
- Intergenerational studies, mission trips, ministry actions have parents and their children working and studying together. They not only spend time together so they can talk, but they also automatically have something to talk about.

Whatever churches do with children and teenagers, they need to keep in mind that the conversation is always three-way—parent, child, and church. You can envision this conversation like a triangle with the sides labeled parent, child, and church. But this is not a triangle with three equal sides. Two of the sides are bigger, those labeled parent and child.

> **A word spoken at the right time is like golden apples on a silver tray.**
>
> **—Proverbs 25:11**

The Prayer Focus

God, our Father, You listen to us so often. Help us as we try to listen to You. Help us also to listen to our children and to hear their expressed and often unexpressed needs. Give us the right

words to encourage and affirm our children and their friends.
Thank You for Your 24-7 availability for us to come to You.
Show us how to be parents with open arms, just as You have
taught us to come to You. In Jesus' name we pray, amen.

Parent Adventures

1. In your conversation with other parents, share something you and your child have discussed recently. Don't reveal your child's secrets. The goal is for parents to encourage one another to listen to their children.

2. Share ideas with other parents about ways to begin conversations with kids the age of yours. This is clearly a bigger topic for parents of teenagers than for parents of preschoolers, but establishing times of listening to your children when they are young may last a lifetime.

3. Ask your children if they have topics they would like to discuss or questions they'd like to ask you. Assure them that they can talk with you about anything (if they can).

4. Review the examples of what churches are doing in this chapter. Knowing that *church* means believers working together as God has gifted them, try inserting your name instead of the word *church* or the leader's name. Which forms of encouraging parent-child conversations might God be asking you to consider helping your church experience?

QUESTIONS FOR DISCUSSION

1. When do children have opportunities to speak and to ask questions at your church? Who listens to them? What are some general topics they are discussing that parents need to know?

2. In what ways do preschoolers, children, and teenagers in your church have opportunities for leadership? How can they take appropriate roles in praying, expressing ideas and concerns, speaking, teaching, and leading worship?

3. Schools have homework hotlines so parents can keep up with their children's assignments. What would a church homework hotline look like if church leaders and parents partnered together? What would be the benefits for children?

4. Think about teenagers at your church. How many do you know by name? How many would name you as an adult who has made a significant investment in their life personally and spiritually? How can your church work together to foster deeper relationships between children and adults?

Chapter 11

Crisis Support

I have told you these things so that in Me you may have
peace. You will have suffering in this world. Be courageous!
I have conquered the world.

—JOHN 16:33

Mike Landry became pastor of Sarasota Baptist Church in June. That October a family crisis occurred that rocked their entire community. In September a family that had recently moved from Texas visited their church. An Evangelism Explosion team from Sarasota Baptist went to visit them. They met the husband and wife, their two teenage daughters, and their quadruplet babies. Mike recalls, "One of our EE teams went to visit them and found out they were Christians. The wife said that she was being stalked by her ex-husband and that he was planning to murder her. About seven weeks later she was found dead at her home."

This family was going through an unimaginable crisis. Sarasota Baptist had a new pastor, and the church was just getting to know this family. Yet, "our church rallied," Mike added. They were called to minister to the family on Friday night. "Immediately we had people from our church come to their home, took the children, and because we weren't sure who the murderer was, our preschool director took the babies to her home. The press would be asking 'where did they go?' 'Somebody from our church has got them.' They stayed there for the next week and a half while police were investigating the murder. The two teenage daughters went to another home. The dad who was broken over the whole thing stayed at a staff member's home. At the time we weren't sure if they were also targets." In addition, the murder attracted significant media attention locally and nationally.

"I went to our congregation Sunday morning. I said, 'Look, something has happened in our church family. You've heard about it on the news. These are our people. We need people who can watch the kids, who can provide meals for the kids and all the relatives who will be coming in. We need to make sure we have people available who can do a myriad of things.' We didn't have any network to do that in place at that time. I said, 'If you're willing to do anything, write it on a piece of paper, what you can do and when you're available. Give us your phone number and bring it up to me.'"

Mike challenged the church to step up and care for the family during this crisis. At the time the church had about five hundred people in attendance. At the end of the service that Sunday, Mike had five hundred pieces of paper in his pocket. One of their staff members organized the church's plan to help this family, and for the next three weeks Sarasota Baptist had people on a rotation twenty-four hours a day doing different things and taking care of them.

Mike recalls the implications that went beyond that family "that so impacted the community because of the press. They kept interviewing us over and over again. They were asking, 'Why would you do this for somebody who has just started coming to your church?' Because we care. 'Why would you help people that you hardly even know? And you're providing food and lodging and you're hiding the kids.'"

The care the church exhibited to this family they barely knew was a witness to the community that brought honor to the kingdom of God. Mike recounted, "I would get phone calls from pastors up and down the Gulf Coast wanting to thank us for being like that. People were coming back to their churches because they had heard my testimony about how our people were stepping up to the plate and ministering to this family." People who had left said, "If this is the way church is now, I want to go back. And they were going back and visiting churches. So it impacted all the churches in the area."

Sarasota Baptist was already an evangelistic church. Because people mobilized for ministry, they had increased opportunities to witness in their community. On a practical level, pastoral transitions take time. Mike knows the blessing this was for him as pastor. Normally, "it takes a while to build credibility. All of a sudden I'm in the forefront. They see me as taking that kind of lead and representing the church well. All of a sudden they're willing to follow my leadership immediately. And then the rest is history."

The history Mike is referring to was not that the church hung on to that moment, but they used it as a turning point that shaped the church. Sarasota Baptist Church is one of few churches in the United States that have been effective in evangelism over the long term. The effectiveness is seen in large numbers attending as well as in how mobilized the church is in evangelism when their total membership is compared to the number of baptisms each year. For ten straight years the ratio of members to baptisms at Sarasota has been less than 20 to 1. In 2007, LifeWay Research recognized this long-term evangelistic effectiveness by calling Sarasota Baptist a "Standout Church."

The crisis that this family at Sarasota Baptist faced was extreme. While the church was not necessarily prepared, they responded without hesitation. While churches cannot anticipate every kind of crisis or pain that families may face, we believe that churches can take steps to prepare to be there for families.

We shared in chapter 5 that parents in America struggle, as we do, with sharing painful family situations with our kids. Every day parents struggle with these questions. Do they tell their kids when Dad has lost his job and they just can't afford camp this summer? Do they explain that the job loss is really hard on Mom and Dad? When the news on the television is bad, do they explain it to their kids or turn off the television? When the family faces death or a debilitating illness, do they explain to the kids or try to hide reality from them? Do parents let kids know when their marriage is going through a tough time?

> **About three out of four parents said they try to keep their own pain away from their children.**

That's telling children about a parent's pain. But what about trying to protect kids from their own pain and disappointment. On television we frequently see stories about a mom who used the Internet to disparage a teenage rival to her daughter's cheerleading tryouts or the dad who gets in a fight at a ballpark when his kid doesn't get to play enough or gets what the dad thinks is a bad call. Teachers tell about helicopter parents who are always hovering to make sure their kids get attention, good grades, and ample opportunities.

Most of the time for most families, life is good. Pain is not the dominant theme for most of us. One way to prepare kids to deal with the inevitable pain and crises of life is to let them see glimpses of others' pain.

"How do you get teenagers to clean house, do laundry, take care of kids, cut the grass, or rake leaves?" Cindy Thiele laughs and says, "You let them get involved in ministry, doing the chores for someone in crisis."

When Pam Mason was pregnant with her fifth child, she discovered that she had cancer. That began a four-year journey for church members that spread to other churches and to members of the community.

Pam and her husband Kerry were members (he still is) of Northeast Church, a nondenominational church in Hendersonville, Tennessee. When the news of Pam's diagnosis spread, the entire church responded. Over time more and more people got involved.

Cindy says that people all over the community got to know one another through the joint ministry. She remembers taking a meal one day and being greeted at the door by a teenager who was home-schooled and free to offer assistance when most adults were working and most kids were in school.

Cindy's two kids, Audrey and Eric, were among teenagers who regularly helped out at the Mason home. Pam would make a list of how they could help—mowing the yard, cleaning the house, doing the dishes, or any other tasks they could do.

The Masons' faith was strong and a witness to everyone who came to minister to them. Some kids thought about death for the first time, and Cindy says that everyone involved grew closer to God and to one another through this ministry.

Pam had a wish that before she died her family would move from an older home to a new one, so the Masons bought a new house. The Northeast Church family packed them up, moved them, and unpacked and put everything in its place. Two weeks later they were gathered together again for Pam's funeral.

Cindy says, "Everyone who ministered to this family received a blessing. I wish the end of the story were different, but we all—both adults and teenagers—grew through this experience."

How Churches Are Responding

Since there is no shortage of pain and disappointment among families today, this is an area where churches can help parents. Churches are already doing this in a number of ways.

First, people within these churches have positioned their church to help by partnering with parents all along. Beginning with young preschoolers, they have established a relationship with parents. Parents and ministers or age-group leaders are more likely to have trust in each other. Those who work with kids at church are more likely to notice when a child acts out in unusual ways. Because they already have a relationship, those church leaders or ministers can go to parents and say: "Your son is behaving differently. He seems upset. Is something going on? How can I help?" Parents are often relieved and grateful to have the pastor or another minister walk alongside them when families face a difficult situation.

On July 28, 2006, sixteen-year-old Nathan Johnson died in a head-on collision with a cement truck. Nathan had a lifetime of evangelism in his few years on earth. All of his family are people of great faith, and that faith has seen them through the difficult hours, days, weeks, and months since Nathan's death.

They've had tremendous support from their own churches and from other churches in their community. Ten or twelve ministers came to the hospital. They comforted family members, friends, and even one another.

Chris, Nathan's father, wanted to talk about the extended care that has been provided, especially in the area of counseling. One of the ministers was Matthew's youth pastor. Matthew is Nathan's younger brother, who was fourteen when Nathan died. The two have had multiple conversations since that time. Andrew, Nathan's older brother, is (and was) a student at Samford University in Birmingham. His college pastor talked with him the day Nathan died, came to the funeral, and met with him at least weekly for the first year after Nathan's death. And a neighboring church has provided free professional counseling for Chris and Kathy, Nathan's mom, as well as for Matthew. Chris and Kathy met with the counselor weekly for the first year and continue to meet with a counselor from time to time.

The love and support from their churches and from neighboring churches has made a significant difference in helping the Johnson family deal with this crisis.

Churches also prepare families for difficult times through their ongoing Bible studies and life applications. Crises can test a person's faith. Having a good foundation in the faith and a daily walk with Jesus Christ can make a difference in getting through the tough situations of life.

Building a family on a foundation of faith is wise. That's Jesus' teaching in His parable of the wise and foolish builders: "Therefore, everyone who hears these words of Mine and acts on them will be like a sensible man who built his house on the rock. The rain fell, the rivers rose, and the winds blew and pounded that house. Yet it didn't collapse, because its foundation was on the rock. But everyone who hears these words of Mine and doesn't act on them will be like a foolish man who built his house on the sand. The rain fell, the rivers rose, the winds blew and pounded that house, and it collapsed. And its collapse was great!" (Matt. 7:24–27).

The builders didn't build the house during the storm. They built it to withstand the storms when they come. And storms are inevitable in everyone's life. Churches partner with parents in building a strong foundation of faith so that, with God's help, you and your kids can withstand the storms of life.

Psalm 44 begins with a generation voicing that they heard the type of testimonies the parents in Psalm 78:4 promised to tell.

"God, we have heard with our ears—our forefathers have told us—the work You accomplished in their days, in days long ago" (Ps. 44:1). Most of the chapter is characterized as "Israel's Complaint" because it details the crises this generation was experiencing. They experienced rejection, humiliation, mockery, ridicule, and disgrace. However, because their forefathers established a foundation of faith in their families, they did not turn their back on God. Psalm 44:17 says, "All this has happened to us, but we have not forgotten You or betrayed Your covenant." What more could we desire for our children than for them to respond to real pain and suffering with such unshaken faith in God? This faith came from hearing of God's provision from their parents, grandparents, and their community of faith.

> Too often we give children answers to remember rather than problems to solve.
>
> —Author Roger Lewin

Churches help parents reduce the risk of having to deal with some tough issues and by helping them plan and prepare for other issues by having special events for parents, beginning either with prenatal parenting classes or with church-parent partnership classes at the time of baby dedication and continuing from there.

Churches can offer child-development training sessions for parents just as they do for age-group leaders, and sometimes churches can offer sessions for parents and age-group leaders together. This is a great time to address in advance some of the painful issues kids face. Not only are parents then more prepared to deal with some of the tough times, but they also realize that they are not alone in helping their children through some difficult issues. Through such church-supported training parents can connect and draw support from one another as well as from church leaders.

Churches acknowledge pain and difficult circumstances in the lives of these members and in people in their community and throughout the world through ministry actions. Children can be included in ministry actions from a young age, doing more as they get older. Here are a few ideas for ways families can minister together through the church:

- Some churches plan family mission and/or ministry trips and provide ways for all ages to serve.
- Families can adopt a widow.
- Families can volunteer to serve at their church's Room in the Inn ministry or at a local soup kitchen.
- Families can shop for school supplies together for families who don't have money to buy what they need. Many churches organize the collection of supplies for families or to be given directly to schools. One such church is the Northern Range Campus of Crossroads Community Church. They held a Backpack Drive for an underprivileged elementary school in Commerce City, Colorado.
- Almost every church has a weekly prayer list of church members and their friends and relatives who are experiencing some kind of family crisis—illness, death, job loss, parent or child away on military assignment, new baby in the family. On an age-appropriate basis, parents can talk with their children about these needs and call their attention to times of intercessory prayer at church. Then parents can pray at home with their children about these concerns. This is especially meaningful when the child knows the person with the need, but children can be taught to pray for the concerns of the church family and not just for the people they know. Praying for people in crisis may also be accompanied by family ministry to meet specific needs.

Families can have great discussions before and after ministry experiences. Churches can provide discussion starters to help parents begin the conversations.

The more the church can offer parents before crisis strikes, the more families are prepared to deal with difficult issues, pain, and disappointment. And the more ministry parents and church leaders have experienced together, the greater the trust and the greater the opportunity to minister when times are hard.

> Common sense is not a spiritual gift.
>
> –Clara Mae Van Brink, preschool director

One way churches help prepare parents is through preaching sermons or sermon series about parenting or about issues that help families and individuals deal with crises in life. Kevin Wendt, a pastor at Concordia Church who focuses on missions, outreach, and evangelism says, "Why do we preach about parenting? It's important for us to stay relevant to our society, and this is one approach we choose to use. How can you have a relevant ministry and not speak to where your people are living right now? We are associated with a day school, and a lot of families with young children are in our church. In the fall when school is starting up and in the spring when school is wrapping up for the year, a lot of families who are considering enrolling their children in the school will come to visit a church worship service. This is a great opportunity to reach these families. So we plan fall and spring sermon series that are geared toward topics of marriage, family, and parenting. Of course, even though we have parents and families in mind, the overall principles that are shared relate to individuals of all ages, not just to parents.

"One parenting series had an open-ended title for each week: 'I wanted a biblical family, but I got . . .' This series brought to light the clash between the sense of idealism that conflicts with the reality of how hard it is to parent, the struggle of children to be godly. Our goal in this series and others is to bring the gospel to bear in a hopeful way even when dysfunction surfaces in the family. The key verse for this series was Psalm 68:6: 'God provides homes for those who are deserted. He leads out the prisoners to prosperity, but the rebellious live in a scorched land.'"

The feedback Kevin has received has been overwhelming. The sermon series on godly parenting clearly hit a need. The people responded to the real hope that is found in Jesus Christ. The hope of the gospel is translated into day-to-day living and day-in and day-out encouragement. And the series seems to connect with both believers and unbelievers who attend, opening a door that might lead to salvation. Preachers don't have to perpetuate the idea that they, or members of their church, are perfect or have everything figured out. The reality of the struggle and the reality of the hope in Christ help them connect and reach the people in their community.

The Prayer Focus

> *God, our Father, thank You for Your Son, our Savior, who showed us how to care for all people, to be moved by people's pain, and to meet people's needs. Help us to love others as You have taught us to love and to teach our children to see the world through Your eyes of love. We ask this because we know that You are love and that all love comes from You. In the name of the One who taught us how to live, Jesus the Christ, amen.*

Parent Adventures

1. Who do you know who is in pain or crisis or has a need? How can you work as a family to minister to that person,

family, or group? Do you need to partner with other families in meeting that need?

2. Parents in pain over problems with children often feel alone, isolated in dealing with difficult issues. Pray for families in pain or crisis. Ask God to reveal ways to encourage the parents.

3. Are you investing in relationships with other Christian parents in a Sunday school class, small group, or affinity group so that you are in position to help other families and be helped if a need arises?

QUESTIONS FOR DISCUSSION

1. List transitional struggles of preschoolers, children, and teenagers that many families have. Brainstorm ways parents and church leaders can partner to prepare parents in advance to be ready to deal with age-related struggles.

2. Share ideas about age-appropriate ways to let children know about family pain—the death of a family member or friend, a parent's job loss, or serious illness of a parent or grandparent, for example.

3. Discuss age-appropriate ways to talk with a child about natural disasters, acts of war or terrorism, church conflict or crisis, the arrest of someone they know (such as a church member or neighbor).

4. How are preschoolers, children, and teenagers given opportunities to see needs in their community and around the world? What opportunities do they have for hands-on ministry? How can families minister together? How can the church plan ways for families to do ministry?

Chapter 12

Rejoice!

Rejoice in the Lord always. I will say it again: Rejoice!

—PHILIPPIANS 4:4

Psalm 100:1 says, "Shout triumphantly to the LORD, all the earth." The King James Version may better capture celebrations of children and teenagers, even in worship: "Make a joyful noise unto the LORD." Christ-followers have many reasons to rejoice, to praise God, and to celebrate His goodness.

In Genesis, God rested from His creation and said it was good. In Genesis He also established the family. Churches can celebrate with families. They can help parents and children celebrate together what God is doing in their lives as children grow even as Jesus grew, "in wisdom and stature, and in favor with God and with people" (Luke 2:52).

Before we look at ways churches are celebrating with families, let's learn what parents think about the celebratory side of parenting. Since we naturally celebrate those things that we consider victories or accomplishments, LifeWay Research began by asking parents how they defined *success* for their kids. The most common definitions parents had for success were if their kids grow up to have good values, are happy, are successful in life, are good people, get a college degree, and are independent adults.

Parents' opinions about what defines success varied depending on how religious the parents are. If parents attend church frequently, they are more likely to emphasize faith in God and being a good person in their definition even though only 24 percent said their children's faith is a mark of parenting success. In fact, only 46 percent of evangelicals mentioned a child's faith in God as a definition of successful parenting.

The lack of a strong emphasis on faith in parents' definition of *success* may show a disconnect between faith and life application. These parents may be involved in church and religious activities but

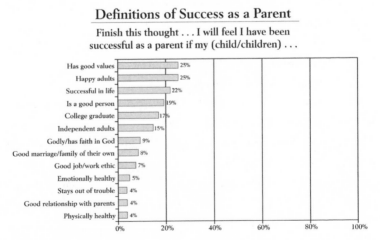

Figure 1. Definitions of Success as a Parent

not necessarily integrating faith into their daily lives, depending on God, seeking God's will, seeking to grow as Christians and to become missional Christians with a Christian worldview that makes all of life based on faith and their relationship with Jesus Christ.

Surveyed parents were asked to define their own success as parents by completing the sentence, "I will have been successful as a parent if my child/children . . ." Here are some of the responses parents gave.

I will have been successful as a parent if my child . . .

- grows up loving God and graduates college.
- grows up to be a better person than me.
- is satisfied, healthy, and happy in what he chooses to do.
- develops a personal relationship with the Lord Jesus Christ and follows His leading.
- grows up loving God, loving herself, and loving others.
- is happy, successful, and at peace with herself and her life.
- grows up and learns how to take care of himself.
- becomes a decent person.
- becomes a good parent to his own children.
- stands on her own, is good to others, is happy with her choices in life, votes, and, most of all, follows God as He leads her.
- lives life with integrity and a code of honor.
- completes school and is well mannered.
- has a good job, marries a good man, and never uses drugs.
- becomes a doctor.
- does well in school and life and stays out of jail. I would like him to be respectful also.
- is a contributor to society.
- is able to get an education and/or a job in order to support herself.
- holds to the values I taught her.

- graduates from school and gets a decent job.
- tells me so.
- grows up to be a free-speaking Christian lady with good moral values and a good work ethic.
- makes it to adulthood alive, with no arrest record.
- outlives me.
- is happy and grows up to be a good, loving, loyal, honest, giving, caring, strong person.
- follows God's will for his life.

Children who succeed in life give parents another reason to celebrate.

One of the ways parents encourage success is to celebrate times when their children take steps in the right direction. Positive reinforcement occurs at the moments when a preschooler shares a toy, a school-age child doesn't hit back, an adolescent chooses not to follow the crowd, and a teenager begins to serve in church.

How parents define success is critical. If this view does not reflect God's view, then both the parents and the children are in for some empty realizations.

Solomon sought after many things and had the power and wealth to try each to the greatest extent. Solomon pursued:

- Wisdom, knowledge, and education
- Pleasure, enjoyment, and laughter
- Achievements, possessions, and wealth
- Work and skills
- Sayings, proverbs, and books

How many of these ideas look similar to parents' responses to success on the previous pages?

After applying himself to these things, Solomon concluded, "When all has been heard, the conclusion of the matter is: fear God and keep His commands, because this is for all humanity" (Eccles. 12:13).

Take a closer look at why Solomon concluded that walking with God rather than other forms of success was desirable. Solomon realized:

- Education ended in grief (Eccles. 1:18).
- Laughter turned out to be madness (Eccles. 2:2).
- Accomplishments and achievements proved there was nothing to be gained (Eccles. 2:11).
- Work and one's occupation lead to no rest (Eccles. 2:23).
- Even making books leads to weariness (We can relate!) (Eccles. 12:12).

Celebrating the right things, celebrating the little things that lead to walking with God make for a joy-filled home. Solomon saw this and included it in his proverbs.

My son, if your heart is wise, my heart will indeed rejoice.
My innermost being will cheer when your lips say what is
    right. (Prov. 23:15–16)

The father of a righteous son will rejoice greatly,
And one who fathers a wise son will delight in him.
Let your father and mother have joy,
and let her who gave birth to you rejoice. (Prov. 23:24–25)

How Churches Are Responding

The mission of the church is found in the Great Commission. Jesus' last words to His disciples instructed them to go and tell others about Him, to share the good news. When people hear and respond to the gospel, the good news, that's reason to celebrate. As children and youth make the decision to follow Christ as Savior and Lord, that's the main reason to celebrate. Churches are also finding many more reasons to celebrate with parents and children along the way.

Legacy Milestones

Many churches celebrate milestones in the development of children in their church. Brian Haynes, associate pastor of marriage and families at Kingsland Baptist Church in Katy, Texas, leads a milestones ministry with his church. The Milestones ministry fits right in with the church's mission statement: "Kingsland's quest is to love God, love people, and equip the generations one home at a time!"

Brian says that Milestones began out of his own personal struggle. As a church leader and a parent, when the time came for him to dedicate his first child to the Lord, he felt inadequate in knowing exactly the steps to take in order to equip his own child to become a Christian and then grow in discipleship, as well as other areas of life. He readily accepted responsibility for caring for his child and directing his child's life, but accepting responsibility didn't mean he knew every step to take. He decided that if he was a minister and wasn't sure about what to do, then probably other parents in his church felt the same way.

Brian started reading and found help as he read. He found a lot to think about. As a Christian educator, he began to apply what he was reading to teachable moments in his child's life. Then he began to think about milestones in family life and ways to integrate church and home. And that's how Kingsland's Legacy Milestones ministry was born.

Milestones is a discipleship process. Twice a year the church holds a parent summit to help parents enter this ministry with their families. Parents can enter the Milestones ministry at the appropriate point for their child. They begin the process by attending one of these summits. The first event drew 150 parents. Now each biannual event draws three to five hundred parents. The summit connects all the parts of Milestones and encourages family devotions. The success of Milestones is based on the understanding that parents are their children's primary faith trainers and that the church's job is to equip and provide resources to help parents in their parenting adventure.

Brian began with a survey, asking parents about family needs, family growth and development needs, and spiritual growth needs. More than a thousand parents completed the survey. At that time only 17 percent were doing any type of family devotion, even once a month. Brian saw a need and an opportunity to teach parents to lead times of worship in their families. He saw an opportunity for Christian discipline in the home.

He began to teach parents to have weekly devotions in the home. The devotions are designed to lead children to the next milestone. Some devotions capitalize on teachable moments. Some build on something that was taught at church recently. The goal is to combine the instruction to parents in Deuteronomy 6:6–7 with the good news of the gospel in a partnership between church and homes.

Change didn't happen overnight among the parents at Kingsland Baptist Church. Brian's work began by helping parents to see the need to have the family devotions. It required a shift in parents' thinking from the church as primary discipler to having parents take the lead in discipleship with their children. Even though they, like the vast majority of parents in the LifeWay Research survey, agreed that their children's spiritual formation was the parents' responsibility, many had determined that they were doing their job by taking their children to church. Brian wanted to help them see that they could do more.

Brian developed a plan that had three parts. First, he wanted to help parents see that the best way to help their children is to grow in their own understanding of the Bible and in their relationship with Jesus Christ. The next step for Brian was to teach parents to lead age-appropriate family devotions in their homes. And finally, he wanted to help parents equip their children for the milestones they face in life, milestones that give families reasons to celebrate.

They chose the name Legacy Milestones because the goal is for parents to leave a legacy of faith for their children and to equip them to own that faith and to keep passing it on from one generation to the next.

The church and parents partner in equipping parents to focus on six milestones. All of Kingland's events, seminars, and processes are now designed to support the Milestones pathway. The milestones are:

Milestone 1. Parent/Baby Dedication

Milestone 2. Salvation and Baptism

Milestone 3. Preparing for Adolescence

Milestone 4. Purity for Life

Milestone 5. Rite of Passage (from childhood to adulthood)

Milestone 6. High School Graduation

Each milestone has an assigned staff member, an event from children or students, and a parenting seminar. Seminars are held twice a year. Some of the events are held at designated times; others, such as salvation and baptism, will occur depending on the child. Events are times of celebration. Here are the events that go with each milestone:

Milestone 1. Parent/Baby Dedication

Milestone 2. Baptism

Milestone 3. Road Trip (a retreat for fourth and fifth graders)

Milestone 4. True Love Waits Commitment Ceremony

Milestone 5. Rite of Passage Ceremony

Milestone 6. Senior Summit

Each milestone also has a seminar for parents:

Milestone 1. First Steps

Milestone 2. How to Lead Your Child to Christ

Milestone 3. Preparing for Adolescence

Milestone 4. Purity for Life

Milestone 5. Preparing My Student for Adulthood

Milestone 6. Preparing My Student to Leave Home[1]

The church provides a resource list for parents and for family devotions specific to each milestone. They also offer parents a suggested outline for leading family devotions.

Most church leaders know they need to help parents disciple their children, but they aren't sure what to do. Brian encourages church leaders to explore a variety of strategies and to develop their own. To learn more about Milestones at Kingsland Baptist Church, go to the Web site at Legacymilestones.com.[2]

Preparation for change takes away the fear. Families at Kingsland are preparing well for milestones and taking the time to celebrate each one.

Annual Milestones

Some other churches have a Milestones ministry that is taking shape in another way. The Milestones ministry at First Baptist Church, Lewisville, Texas, has a goal to celebrate with children and students and their parents each year, from pregnancy through college, with a milestone event. The church's children's ministry, led by Wayne Cotton, and the student ministry, led by Mikel Hatfield, work together to provide milestone events for children through students. The milestones fit right in with the goals of both ministries. The children's ministry has a mission statement: "To equip parents and volunteers to impact eternity through reaching and teaching children about Jesus." The student ministry is called "2.10" because of the impact of one verse of Scripture, Ephesians 2:10: "For we are His creation—created in Christ Jesus for good works, which God prepared ahead of time so that we should walk in them."[3]

Some milestone events are the responsibility of the children's ministry, some are the responsibility of the student ministry, and everyone works together on some events. For example, when sixth graders move into the seventh grade, the ministries work together to plan a meeting for parents to help them get to know one another, to provide a smooth transition for children, and to help parents know how the church will relate to their students.

The milestones ministry is a part of the church's Christian education ministry in which all the age groups are working together to focus on the home as the primary place of Christian discipleship. The goals are to keep children, students, and young adults involved in church and in a growing relationship with Jesus Christ; to help parents be the primary resource for their children's discipleship; and to aid in deepening parent-child relationships. They also expect to see parents grow as believers because of their role in teaching their children. Teaching in adult Sunday school departments will also help parents understand their role in directing the spiritual formation of their children.

Among the milestones are parent/baby dedication, a family blessing where parents pray and bless their children, an event to give children a Bible with parents writing a note for that event, a ceremony for children moving into the student area, a family camping trip, a manners class for parents and children, a family retreat, and a journaling class for parents and children. Some of the events are more instructional in nature, and some are purely celebrative. Children and students will still have age-group events, but more events will draw parents and children together rather than separate them.[4]

Both of these Texas churches—Kingsland in Katy and First Baptist in Lewisville—are celebrating with parents the milestones of their children's lives. And they're basing those celebrations on the eternal Word of God. Now that's the type of celebration that has a real and lasting impact!

In addition to events that center on milestones, churches have the opportunity to set aside time for parents to encourage one another. For over ten years First Baptist Church, Smyrna, Tennessee, has had an event whose sole purpose is to celebrate God's gift of marriage. The annual evening is called "Romance and Roses." Couples tell their stories of inspiration. One year there might be a young couple sharing something they have overcome such as an illness. We've also heard a couple simply share how their marriage has grown in the Lord through sixty-three years together. There is always plenty of laughter as the evening is light and an encouragement for couples to continue enriching their marriages for the Lord. But the primary focus of the night is to celebrate.

Those within the church also have opportunities to help parents rejoice each and every week as they interact with children and their parents. This encouragement along the way is just as important as the more comprehensive milestone plans. KyAnne Weaver, children's and family life director at Pocono Community Church, models celebrating the things that matter to God that she sees in kids' lives.

KyAnne recently met with her son's cross-country coach and resisted the urge to get caught up in speculating on his running potential. Instead, she made sure the coach knew her priority was her son's character. She told him, "We love sports. My husband and I were involved in sports. But I have to tell you for my youngest son that I would rather push character than winning the race or being the best athlete."

In her role at church, KyAnne also encourages other parents to celebrate good character. "I am always telling parents, 'Watch their character. When you see something in their character like Jesus, let them know how much you appreciate seeing that in them as the Lord works in them.'"

As parents are picking up their children on Sundays, KyAnne looks for opportunities to say things like, "Your son is so kind. If there is a new kid, he is always looking out for others. He is already living out Philippians 2, and he is eight. That's awesome! I know he may act immature and be struggling with his grades, but he is really looking out for other people, and you need to tell him that, because that's better than being an all 'A' student."

The parenting adventure is filled with large and small reasons to celebrate. Watch for these moments and milestones in your children's lives.

We began this book with God's instructions to families found in Deuteronomy 6: "These words that I am giving you today are to be in your heart. Repeat them to your children. Talk about them when you sit in your house and when you walk along the road, when you lie down and when you get up" (Deut. 6:6–7). Let's end with another instruction from God in the same book: "You are to feast there in the presence of the LORD your God and rejoice with your family" (Deut. 14:26). And a verse from the New Testament, "Rejoice in the Lord always. I will say it again: Rejoice!" (Phil. 4:4).

The Prayer Focus

God, we confess that our prayers are often more filled with needs than praises and that our praises are not always for the things You value most. We are truly thankful for Your gifts to us and to our families.
Help us to teach our children to celebrate life, to know the joy of thanking You, and to desire to follow You all their days. You are the One who gives life meaning, and we want our children to know that. We love You and Your Son, and we pray in His name. Amen.

Parent Adventures

1. Partner with one or more families with children the age of yours and celebrate together a milestone in your children's lives.

2. This week, when you tuck your children in bed at night, share praises from the day. Make this a daily habit in your own prayer life.

3. Share with another parent some ways God has blessed your family recently. Whether the other parent has more concerns or praises, voice a prayer for both of your families.

QUESTIONS FOR DISCUSSION

1. Brainstorm some ways your church can partner with parents to celebrate growth and transitions in your children's lives.

2. How does your church communicate success to children? Brainstorm ways to communicate that success is doing what God wants you to do.

3. How does your church celebrate—in worship on a regular basis, when children are dedicated, when children are baptized, when people return from a mission trip? What truths do these celebrations communicate to children? What truths should they communicate? How can church celebrations accomplish that?

Epilogue

The Adventure Continues

"Run with endurance the race that lies before us."

—HEBREWS 12:1

O ne of our family's favorite authors is C. S. Lewis. In the last scene of *The Lion, the Witch and the Wardrobe*, the Pevensie children have just returned from an exhilarating array of adventures in Narnia. They have found their way back to the professor's house. After absorbing this reality, they ask the professor, "Will we ever return to Narnia?" He assures them that although traveling through the wardrobe might be over, many more adventures await them in Narnia.

Wherever you are on this parenting adventure, we assure you, you have many more adventures awaiting you. You might not "get there" the same way, but adventures wait for you nonetheless. Exciting? Absolutely! Dangerous? Often. But God, who is the author and giver of the adventure of life, will be with you on all of them. Trust in Him. Rest in Him. Run after Him.

John 1 contains the story of Jesus noticing two men following Him. He turns and in typical Jesus fashion asks a thought-provoking question: "What are you looking for?" (v. 38). Throughout this study we have encouraged you to include God in your parenting, to talk with Him and seek His guidance in every aspect of your parenting experience—from, "Thank You, Lord, this is going great right now," to, "Help me, Lord, I think I'm going crazy with this thirteen-year-old!" and everything in between. Through all of your parenting adventures, what if He were to ask you, "What are you looking for?" How would you respond?

As your adventure continues, what do you want out of your parenting experience? What do you think God wants to accomplish through you and your family? What are you looking for?

One Parent's Adventure Begins

As your children leave for their own adventure with God, your life as parents is far from over. You may be tempted to recline in that easy chair or collapse on the couch for a much-needed rest (OK, a short nap is acceptable). The truth is, God has many more adventures awaiting you. Here is Nan Williams' story:

> When I was seventeen, I felt God calling me to missions. My husband and I married almost five years later. We were both busy serving in churches and time went by. We went to a missionary appointment service for some friends going to Thailand to serve. During the service, I felt God saying, "Now is the time." I told God I couldn't go now because my baby (he was twenty-three) needed me, and God told me clearly that He would take care of my son. I thought, I can't go now, Lord, my parents are close to eighty. God

told me again that He would take care of my parents better than I could. About that time, my husband said to me, "It's time." We stepped out on faith and almost to the date, one year later, we were appointed to the mission field to serve in Tanzania."[1]

Whether the next step of your journey is to missions or some other work God calls you to do, you can rest assured that God loves you and your children more than you can ever imagine. And just as we have pointed out throughout this book, God cares about you in your parenting role. He has provided ways that parents and churches can partner together to bring up children "in the training and instruction of the Lord" (Eph. 6:4).

Where Do Parents Stand and What Can Churches Do?

When you see the image of Mom and Dad standing in the driveway waving good-bye to Junior as he pulls away in an over-loaded car with all his stuff, headed to college, tears are always part of the scene. The question is, are those tears of regret, relief, reluctance, or pure joy? Are parents ready for the empty nest? Do they want to move on to the next stage of their lives, or do they cling to the daily demands of parenting a child or teenager in the home? Let's see what we can learn from the parenting survey from LifeWay Research.

According to the survey of more than twelve hundred parents, just over half of all parents look forward with excitement to the day their kids grow up and are ready to face the world on their own. Thirty-four percent think of this day with fear and worry over whether they'll be ready, while 15 percent say the empty nest is simply too painful to consider.

As Jay Strother, minister to emerging generations at Brentwood Baptist Church near Nashville, pointed out (see chapter 8), this is a real ministry opportunity for churches. Parents who face their kids' future with fear and worry need a relationship with Jesus Christ. Those who are already Christians need to mature in their faith. Not that some concern over the future isn't normal for some parents, but the church can partner with the parents all the way.

Again, churches can help by reassuring parents of the grace and forgiveness of God available through Jesus Christ. "As far as the east is from the west, so far has He removed our transgressions from us" (Ps. 103:12). "If we confess our sins, He is faithful and righteous to forgive us our sins and to cleanse us from all unrighteousness" (1 John 1:9).

When asked, "Is it hard to focus on long-term goals?" surveyed parents gave a moderate response with just 7 percent strongly agreeing and 18 percent strongly disagreeing. However, a significant minority (43 percent) agree that they have difficulty focusing on long-term goals or strategies for raising their children.

Churches partnering with parents to help them nurture their children in Christian discipleship, like First Baptist Church, Hendersonvillle, Tennessee (see chapter 9), and preparing children for their next milestone, like Kingsland Baptist Church in Katy, Texas (see chapter 11), can help parents look ahead to see what's down the road for their children. Parents may need to be reminded that God has a plan for their lives as well as for their kids' lives. "'For I know the plans I have for you'—this is the LORD's declaration'—plans for your welfare, not for disaster, to give you a future and a hope'" (Jer. 29:11).

We live in an age when churches are trying to reclaim young adults who have dropped out of church. In *Essential Church,* authors Thom S. Rainer and Sam S. Rainer III look at how churches are reaching out to young adults; and through the stories of those young adults, they explore characteristics of churches that make them essential in young adult lives so that they will stay in church because of the difference it makes in their lives.[2] In his book, *In Real Time*, pastor Mike Glenn tells about Kairos worship services at Brentwood Baptist Church near Nashville that target young adults who often are unsaved, unchurched, or unfamiliar with what the Bible says about God, salvation, and life. Many of these young adults grew up in the church but somehow missed learning much about the Bible.[3]

While Brentwood and the churches described in *Essential Church* are doing a wonderful job of reaching and reclaiming young adults, this generation of parents, and the churches that partner with them, have the exciting potential of making a real difference with a generation of children. By being proactive as spiritual formation guides with their children, parents can have confidence that their children will have every opportunity to come to saving faith in Jesus Christ and then continue to grow to become mature Christians as adults who make a difference in their world. Parents who choose not only to accept responsibility for their children's discipleship but also take specific actions to develop a plan for spiritual development already have their guidebook in hand, the Holy Bible, God's eternal Word.

> **The most common definitions parents had for success were if their kids grow up to have good values, are happy, are successful in life, are good people, get a college degree, and are independent adults.**
>
> —LifeWay Research

Survey data has indicated that parents with a plan are more positive about the parenting experience and how well their family is doing. Missional Christians know that their parenting plan is based on the Word of God. Survey results support this. If we compare two respondents identical in every regard except for their familiarity with what the Bible has to say about parenting, this is what we find: a respondent who has no knowledge of what the Bible has to say about parenting has about a 60-percent chance of having some type of parenting plan in place. In contrast, a respondent who is highly knowledgeable about what the Bible says about parenting has about a 77-percent chance of having some type of parenting plan. As familiarity increases, the chances the respondent has a parenting plan increase as well.

Parents who have a plan, overall, have more positive parenting experiences. Parents who do not have a parenting plan, overall, tend to have less positive parenting experiences. Your plan may be as simple as committing to use principles in this book to begin your parenting adventure and to join with other parents at church to encourage one another along the way.

Parents want to take good care of their children, to give them what they need. The goal of churches partnering with parents is that parents "might learn that man does not live on bread alone but on every word that comes from the mouth of the LORD" (Deut. 8:3). Jesus quoted these words when the devil tempted Him to command the stones to become bread to relieve His hunger after His forty days in the wilderness before He began His ministry (see Matt. 4:4). God's changeless Word continues to be essential to parents today.

We've looked at the importance of teaching our children biblical truths. Let's look once again at what the Bible says about this:

> LORD, You light my lamp;
> my God illuminates my darkness.
> With You I can attack a barrier,
> and with my God I can leap over a wall.
> God—His way is perfect;
> the word of the LORD is pure.
> He is a shield to all who take refuge in Him.

For who is God besides the LORD?
And who is a rock? Only our God.
God—He clothes me with strength
and makes my way perfect.

He makes my feet like the feet of a deer
and sets me securely on the heights. (Ps. 18:28–33)

Every word of God is pure;
He is a shield to those who take refuge in Him. (Prov. 30:5)

"Those who hear the word of God and keep it are blessed!"
(Luke 11:28)

Parents with a plan for their children want to "bring them up in the training and instruction of the Lord" (Eph. 6:4). To aid their plan for discipleship, parents can turn to Paul's words in Ephesians 6:10–18:

Finally, be strengthened by the Lord and by His vast
strength. Put on the full armor of God so that you can
stand against the tactics of the Devil. For our battle is not
against flesh and blood, but against the rulers, against
the authorities, against the world powers of this darkness,
against the spiritual forces of evil in the heavens. This is why
you must take up the full armor of God, so that you may be
able to resist in the evil day, and having prepared everything,
to take your stand.

Stand, therefore,
with truth like a belt around your waist,
righteousness like armor on your chest,
and your feet sandaled with readiness for the gospel of peace.
In every situation take the shield of faith,
and with it you will be able to extinguish
the flaming arrows of the evil one.

Take the helmet of salvation,
and the sword of the Spirit, which is God's word.
With every prayer and request, pray at all times in the Spirit,
and stay alert in this.

In Acts 20, Paul was saying good-bye to the Christians at Ephesus. Both Paul and the Ephesians knew that they would likely never see each other face-to-face again. His parting blessing is appropriate for parents, and for their partnering churches: "And now I commit you to God and to the message of His grace, which is able to build you up and to give you an inheritance among all who are sanctified" (Acts 20:32).

What Adventures Await You?

Fast-forward to the end of your life. As people remember you, what do you want said about your life as a parent and as a person?

We've encouraged you to form a game plan, an intentional strategy as you experience the adventure of parenting. But right now, before you make any further plans for today or tomorrow, seek God. Ask Him to shape your parenting dreams and expectations. Let all your plans begin with Him. Let your prayer begin with Him.

Wherever you are in your parenting, just beginning with that newborn, in the trenches (and joys) of the teen years, or on the verge of launching your children from the home, seek the Lord.

Take comfort that the adventure of parenting, with its battles, its challenges, and its responsibilities is not yours alone. God, the Ultimate Parent, has promised never to leave you (see Heb. 13:5). This Parent sent His Son who taught us that "with God all things are possible" (Matt. 19:26).

Whatever you do or plan to do in your parenting adventure, commit it to the Lord, and watch Him work. "Commit your activities to the LORD and your plans will be achieved" (Prov. 16:3). And that will be worth celebrating.

Let the adventure continue!

The Prayer Focus

We began this study with a prayer from Paul found in Ephesians 1. We want to close our time with you with another prayer from Paul found in Ephesians 3. Thank you for investing this time with us.

I pray that He may grant you, according to the riches of His glory, to be strengthened with power through His Spirit in the inner man, and that the Messiah may dwell in your hearts through faith.
I pray that you, being rooted and firmly established in love, may be able to comprehend with all the saints what is the breadth and width, height and depth, and to know the Messiah's love that surpasses knowledge, so you may be filled with all the fullness of God.

Now to Him who is able to do above and beyond all that we ask or think—according to the power that works in you—to Him be glory in the church and in Christ Jesus to all generations, forever and ever. Amen. (Eph. 3:16–21)

Appendix

Definitions

For the parenting survey, LifeWay Research used the following definitions:

Protestants

Those who attend a Protestant church.

Religious Segments

1. Heavy church: typically attend religious worship services weekly.

2. Light church: typically attend religious worship services one to three times a month.

3. Unchurched: attend less than once a month, only on special occasions, or not at all but do have a personal religious identification.

4. Nonreligious: no religious preference, atheist, or agnostic.

Born-Again Christians

Those who have made a personal commitment to Jesus Christ and believe they will go to heaven because they have confessed their sins and accepted Christ as their Savior.

Evangelicals

Born-again Christians who:

- agree that the Bible is the accurate, written Word of God.
- agree that they personally have the responsibility to tell others about their religious beliefs.
- agree that their religious faith is important in their lives.
- agree that God is all-knowing, all-powerful, and rules the universe today.
- agree that salvation is available through grace alone.
- disagree that Jesus committed sins while on earth.
- disagree that Satan is not a living being but just a symbol of evil.

Notes

Chapter 1, The Adventure Begins

1. International Cultic Studies Association, "Teenage Spirituality and the Internet," online at www.icsahome.com/infoserv_articles/lutz_alison_teen agespiritualityandinternet.htm, accessed May 31, 2008.

2. John G. Bruhn, *The Sociology of Community Connections* (New York: Springer, 2004), 6. Online at http://books.google.com/books?id= EsvME8KXXAcC&pg=PT26&lpg=PT26&dq=nothing+is+more+likely+t o+produce+a+happy,+well-adjusted+child+than+a+loving+family.&source =web&ots=uKJ-xl2ioE&sig=UYKqCQ8rU58ZMcqW6TiD8j5ryHw&hl= en. Accessed May 31, 2008.

3. *Social Technologies*, "MTV Research: The Future of Happiness," online at http://www.socialtechnologies.com/mtv.aspx. Accessed May 31, 2008.

Chapter 2, Letting Go

1. Tim Elmore, *Nurturing the Leader within Your Child: What Every Parent Needs to Know* (Nashville: Thomas Nelson, 2001), online at www. growingleaders.com.

Chapter 4, Let's Talk

1. Perry McGuire, "Buzz about 'the talk,'" *HomeLife*, November 2007, 46–47).

2. To go deeper into the issue of busyness, we recommend Michael Zigarelli, *Freedom from Busyness* (Nashville: LifeWay, 2005).

3. See Sheila Gains, *Family Mealtime: A Menu for Opportunities* (Arapahoe County: Colorado State University Extension, 2000). Online at www.ext.colostate.edu/PUBS/columncc/cc000922.html.

4. Learn more about coaching in Jane Creswell, *Christ-Centered Coaching: 7 Benefits for Ministry Leaders* (St. Louis: Lake Hickory Resources, 2006).

Chapter 5, Pain Happens

1. Tony Dungy, *Quiet Strength: The Principles, Practices & Priorities of a Winning Life* (Carol Stream, IL: Tyndale House, 2007), 213.

Chapter 7, The Church's Role

1. Chip Heath and Dan Heath, *Made to Stick: Why Some Ideas Survive and Others Die* (New York: Random House, 2007), 159.

2. The research methodology for the parenting study included a large, representative sample of America. Methodology included control for census data regarding age of respondents, location, etc. Results are highly valid. Data were collected from a representative sample of American adults with children under eighteen years of age in the households surveyed. The national sample size was twelve hundred. Interviews were conducted online with a demographically balanced panel. Respondents were not informed that the survey was being conducted by LifeWay Research. The surveys were conducted in September 2007. A supplement sample of two hundred adults with a child or children under one year old was also surveyed. At a 95-percent confidence level and a 50-percent response distribution, the potential sampling error on the primary national sample is 2.7 percentage points.

3. Telephone interview with Billy Crow, Formosa Baptist Church, Clinton, Arkansas, May 29, 2008.

4. Telephone interview with Jeanne Burns, Ridgecrest Baptist Church, Springfield, Missiouri, May 29, 2008.

5. Telephone interview with Clara Mae Van Brink, Norcross, Georgia, May 21, 2008.

6. Thom S. Rainer and Sam S. Rainer III, *Essential Church* (Nashville: B&H Publishing Group, 2008), 2.

Chapter 8, Planning Together

1. FamilyFEST is sponsored by Woman's Missionary Union (www.wmu.com). The story is from Judi S. Hayes, *Youth on Mission Plan Book, Volume 14* (Birmingham: Woman's Missionary Union, 2008).

2. Thom S. Rainer and Eric Geiger, *Simple Church: Returning to God's Process for Making Disciples* (Nashville: B&H Publishing Group, 2006).

3. Telephone interview with Jay Strother, Brentwood Baptist Church, Nashville, Tennessee, May 23, 2008.

Chapter 9, A Yes Church

1. Telephone interview with Clara Mae Van Brink, Norcross, Georiga, May 21, 2008.

2. Anna B. Warner (1820–1915), "Jesus Loves Me."

3. James Riley Estep Jr., "Biblical Principles for a Theology for Christian Education" in James Estep, Michael Anthony, and Greg Allison, *A Theology for Christian Education* (Nashville: B&H Publishing Group, 2008), 44.

4. Ibid., 51–52.

5. Ibid., 67.

6. Marcia McQuitty, "Teaching Preschoolers," in Rick Yount, *The Teaching Ministry of the Church* (Nashville: B&H Publishing Group, 2008), 298.

7. "RipCord, The Discipleship Strategy of First Baptist Church Student Ministry, Hendersonville, TN," an unpublished paper.

8. Ibid.

9. Ibid.

Chapter 10, Facilitating Conversation

1. Ken Hemphill and Richard Ross, *Parenting with Kingdom Purpose* (Nashville: Broadman & Holman, 2005), 61

2. Telephone interview with Beth Tolar, Northside Baptist Church, West Columbia, South Carolina, May 23, 2008.

3. Thom S. Rainer and Sam S. Rainer III, *Essential Church* (Nashville: B&H Publishing Group, 2008), 124–25.

4. Telephone interview with Bill Newton, First Baptist Church, Lonoke, Arkansas, May 22, 2008. Parents and kids study *Now That I'm a Christian* by William E. Young (Nashville: LifeWay, 1993).

5. Telephone interview with Mikel Hatfield, First Baptist Church, Lewisville, Texas, May 23, 2008.

Chapter 12, Rejoice!

1. Kingsland Baptist Church, Katy, Texas, www.kingsland.org. Accessed May 22, 2008.

2. Telephone interview with Brian Haynes, Kingsland Baptist Church, Katy, Texas, May 23, 2008.

3. First Baptist Church, Lewisville, Texas, www.fbclewisville.org. Accessed May 26, 2008.

4. Telephone interview with Mikel Hatfield, First Baptist Church, Lewisville, Texas, May 23, 2008.

Epilogue, The Adventure Continues

1. Judi S. Hayes, *Youth on Mission, Vol. 14* (Birmingham: Woman's Missionary Union, 2008), 50.

2. Thom S. Rainer and Sam S. Rainer III, *Essential Church* (Nashville: B&H Publishing Group, 2008).

3. Michael L. Glenn, *In Real Time* (Nashville: B&H Publishing Group, 2009).

About the Authors

Scott McConnell

Scott McConnell is associate director of LifeWay Research. He has researched the beliefs, behaviors, needs, and preferences of church leaders, laity, and the unchurched for LifeWay Christian Resources for twelve years. Scott enjoys learning from each group he studies, and he seeks to apply research findings to real-life situations and decisions in church life. His research has addressed a variety of issues by interviewing young adult church dropouts, the formerly churched, standout churches who are effective in evangelism, and multisite churches.

Scott concentrated in marketing and strategic management as he received a bachelor of science degree in economics from the Wharton School of the University of Pennsylvania. He was mentored in sound survey methodology and actionable decision-focused research as an associate project manager at National Analysts, a Philadelphia-based research and consulting firm. Projects included segmentation, satisfaction, and product development research for Fortune 100 telecommunications and utilities companies.

Scott, his wife Debbie, and their two kids, Madison (nine years old) and Max (six years old), live in Nashville, Tennessee. They are actively involved at Hermitage Hills Baptist Church. Scott serves as a deacon and preteen Sunday school teacher and supports the church's multisite efforts.

Rodney and Selma Wilson

Rodney and Selma have been married for thirty-two years and have two adult daughters and one son-in-law. Rodney has served as youth minister, campus minister, collegiate missions director, and for the past ten years has served as marriage and family minister at First Baptist Church, Smyrna, Tennessee.

Selma has served as a ministry partner with Rodney over the years as well as a teacher, social worker, and marriage and family consultant. For the past fourteen years she has served through the ministry of LifeWay Christian Resources through the startup of women's ministry and currently as associate vice president of the Church Resources Division.

Rodney and Selma have been actively involved in marriage and family ministry for most of their married life, teaching, speaking, writing, and counseling to build strong marriages and families as God designed. They have been actively involved in *HomeLife* magazine for the past ten years as contributors and recently served for five years as executive editors. They are the authors of *Extraordinary Marriage* and national speakers for Festivals of Marriage. Their mission is to help marriages and families reach their full potential in Jesus Christ.

For rest and relaxation Rodney and Selma like biking, water and snow skiing, and hiking. Rodney enjoys running and is currently training for his eleventh marathon while Selma prefers a chair on the beach with a good book.